Praise for The Secret Million Dollar Paradigm

"There is a key inside Rachael's book, that when you find it, will unlock the door to help you manifest everything you desire in your life. Study this great book and implement immediately. When you do, you'll experience wonderful magic in your life."

> – Peggy McColl, *New York Times* Best-Selling Author

"I absolutely love *The Secret Million Dollar Paradigm*. What makes it so special are Rachael's own experiences and the stories of other "normal" people who have become self-made millionaires. I suggest you use these ideas and launch into inspired action right away."

> – Nana Jokura, Author of Your Healthy Success

"Rachael Downie's work with this book is extraordinary – herself and a handful of self-made millionaires take you by the hand and show you how to do the same! Learn from those who have DONE it! Get the book, get empowered and go create it for yourself!"

> – Anders Hansen, Illusionist, keynote performer, change-maker, AndersHansen.com

"What sets Rachael apart? She not only knows her stuff, and knows how to help people – she truly cares. I've known Rachael for over a decade. I've trained her, coached her and I'm proud to call her a friend. If you're looking for someone who walks their talk in a world where most are selling empty promises, you'll be wise to listen to what Rachael has to say."

> – Nick Cownie, Success Dynamics Institute, Author of *7 Minute Mindset: How to Eliminate Fear, Procrastination and Failure in 7Minutes Or Less*

"If you're ready to achieve more than ever before and take a quantum leap – then this is the book for you. It offers clear strategies and tools to shift your mindset around money and what's actually possible for you.

> – Nicole Brandes, New Leadership Expert, International Executive Coach, Speaker

"It doesn't matter what cards you get dealt, life is a game made for everyone, and love, joy and fulfillment are the prizes. The interviews and points in this book will open your mind to paradigms and the effect they have on our lives and the perspective of a millionaire mindset!"

> – David Peacock Author of *Awareness, The Groundwork For Fulfillment*, Personal development coach and network marketer.

"**The Secret Million Dollar Paradigm** is so good! What makes it so unique is the use of Rachael's own experiences and other "normal" people who have become self-made millionaires. This is not fiction, this it how's its done. This will inspire you that you have what it takes to do it to.

> – Doug Dane, Speaker and Author

I have had the pleasure of knowing Rachael for the past 2 years. Let me tell you, she is the real deal! This book is a must read! You can feel her genuine and authenticity all throughout her book. This book will inspire you, motivate you, plus give you the tools you need to make your leap!

> – Jacquelyn MacKenzie, International Best Selling Author, *Jacquelyn the Prophet of Profit*

THE SECRET
Million Dollar
PARADIGM

YOUR FORMULA FOR SUCCESS
Featuring Interviews with **Bob Proctor** and other Self-made Millionaires

Rachael Downie

Hasmark
PUBLISHING
INTERNATIONAL

Permission should be addressed in writing to Rachael Downie at
205 Clarendon Rd., Gretna Tasmania, Australia 7140 or
rachael@rachaeldownie.com.au

Editor: Corinne Casazza
corinnecasazza@gmail.com

Cover & Book Design: Anne Karklins
annekarklins@gmail.com

Cover Photo by Tommy Collier
tommycollier.com

ISBN 13: 978-1-989161-75-3
ISBN 10: 1989161758

Hasmark
PUBLISHING
INTERNATIONAL

Dedicated to you and the infinite potential within.

"Everything you believe is true"

ACKNOWLEDGEMENT

I want to thank every person who has contributed to the success of this book. That would mean every person I've come in contact with, who has shaped my life in some way.

To those of you who gave me the opportunity to interview you, I'm so grateful that you said yes and shared your learning's and life experience to help others. It's been a privilege to have met and worked with every single one of you. Keep going with your success. Life keeps getting better and better

Thank you, Doug Dane. You were instrumental in building my new self-image. I am forever grateful for breathing your belief in me and seeing something in me I was completely unaware of.

Thank you to my husband James. I know this journey of me stepping into my life's purpose hasn't been an easy one. It really changed the goal posts for both of us. You are one incredible human being and Dad and I am so thankful for the life that we've created together and continue creating.

To my amazing children, I'm truly blessed to be your Mama. You amaze me with your greatness, individual talents and creative abilities every single day. I'm so proud of all that you are becoming. You are lights in my life every day and I want to be the best parent for you.

My Intention: To inspire others to step into their purpose and show them how to create abundance and prosperity in their lives.

TABLE OF CONTENTS

Part 2: Interviews

Part 3 Daily Rituals for Success

THE MORE MONEY
YOU EARN
THE MORE PEOPLE
YOU CAN HELP.

FOREWORD

I have had the pleasure of knowing Rachael Downie for a number of years now. From the first time I met her I saw someone with a very special understanding of how to move ahead in life while continuing to keep her family the priority. That is a gift that we all can learn from.

In this book you will learn:

– How to change your perception around money and the earning of it.

– How to build a strong self-image, create a healthy relationship with money, and create the life you truly want.

Rachael could very well be just like you… so make sure you do the things she did and watch what will happen in your life. She shows you how to take responsibility for yourself so that you will not be forced to live the life that others impose on you.

This is a book you can take your time with. It is not the kind of book you need to read cover to cover as quickly as possible. Pick it up and read a chapter that is relevant to what you need today. You can sit it on your desk or side table to be picked up often.

This book really does give you the formula to success.

In the second half you will see some quality interviews. I know the majority of these people that Rachael has interviewed and you will be impressed with the quality and material that is in these conversations.

One of the interviews comes from my father, Bob Proctor. I know that I am fortunate to be his son. I have lived all my life knowing this wonderful man and have seen first hand that he really lives the way of life that he teaches. Most mornings my father and I will speak to each other on the phone before anyone else is up. The early morning conversations that we have will always be a blessing in my life. From these conversations I have learned so much and know that I am living a charmed life because of all that he has taught me and more importantly, by applying what he has taught me.

One of the first things we do everyday is to "talk good" about people behind their back. While most of the world seem to be focused on the negative we have decided to focus on the positive. Imagine what a wonderful place this would be if everyday we talked good about people even when they were not listening. That one lesson in itself is worth it's weight in gold. I have learned that when we stay in a positive way of thinking we really do attract wonderful things and wonderful people into our lives. Yes, what we see in the world is really a reflection of how we are.

It has been heart warming for me to read this book by Rachael. If you will take to heart and implement what she discusses in the following chapters I know for a fact that you will start to live a charmed life as well.

Brian Proctor
VP of Business Development, Proctor Gallagher Institute, Author

DEFINITION OF PARADIGM

A paradigm is a multitude of habits that is stored in
your subconscious mind. Almost all of your behaviour is habitual.

If you want to change your results in your life you must
change your paradigm to be in harmony with the success you desire.

INTRODUCTION

This book is a reflection of my breakthroughs over the past 18 months since the word "paradigm" entered my life.

"The only limits in our life are the ones that we impose on ourselves."
– Bob Proctor

I want you to experience the personal breakthrough and freedom I felt when I heard about paradigms. I want you to experience the growth in income, the understanding, the awareness of what is truly possible for you in your life, right now.

My gift to you is sharing my story, my growth and the stories and experiences of six other individuals who experienced changes and growth that allowed them to bring more money, more freedom and true "richness" into their lives.

I want you to be able to experience this.

I want you to crack the code that is stopping you from living a life of abundance and prosperity.

I want you to make more money then you ever imagined possible for yourself. Why? Because the more money you make, the more people you can help and the more freedom you can experience every day.

I made a DECISION when I was younger that I was going to have more in my life. I was going to be successful. I was going to earn a lot of money and I was going to help a lot of people worldwide.

My plan was to get a damn good education and work hard. I did both and it didn't work! I did everything that I had been told to do so why didn't it work?

I've learned more in the past two years about success than I have in the past 24 years of schooling and degrees – and I've done a lot of study!! I was what you'd call a conscious incompetent! What I realise now is knowledge doesn't mean anything if you aren't taking action in alignment with the good you desire. I am really excited to be sharing this with you throughout the chapters so you gain understanding rather than the ignorance I experienced for so long.

I want to help you do what I was able to do over the past two years.

I first realised that I was really dissatisfied with the life I was leading when I was teaching. I learned how stress impacts your health at a professional development course and my mind was opened. I felt like I wasn't making the difference that I could be making in the world. I delved into understanding emotions and their impact on the body, positive and negative. I thought I'd cracked the code to life and understanding and became a life/business coach. But I soon found that I hadn't. I coached people for free – I just wanted to take make their lives better. I received psychic income. I was barely making any money for the service I was providing. This is not uncommon. There are plenty of people out there offering a fabulous service and not asking for payment.

Now it didn't matter that I had invested hundreds of thousands of dollars into my own development and education. I didn't value myself and what I had to offer. I didn't feel worthy and it made me feel really uncomfortable asking for payment.

I went from charging $200 an hour to $1000 an hour in under 18 months because I learned how to change my paradigms, (particularly around my self-image and money) and I can't wait to share how this is possible for you as well.

The mind of a millionaire doesn't think like everyone else's. There is plenty of evidence of that, or making a million would be easy and everyone would be doing it! What is the secret sauce, the recipe?

It's really understanding the mind and becoming aware that what you think about in the conscious mind isn't enough. You need to change what's in harmony with the subconscious mind. It's understanding paradigms and how you can shift yours to change your results. Right now, every single thought you're having is creating the results in your life.

BACKGROUND

Growing up I saw others around me who were "wealthier" than our family. My parents and grandparents would draw attention to people that had money as if to say we weren't like those people. It was a reflection of their beliefs about themselves and money and what had been passed to them from previous generations. I didn't want to be like that. I wanted to create choices for myself. I wanted to be able to afford the car I wanted to drive.

I wanted an abundance of food. I wanted to buy my own home. I wanted to choose the school that was best for my children. I wanted to give back. I wanted to have money and choices.

I grew up hearing, "There isn't enough money, we can't afford it, we have to go without." This became my conditioning to money.

I remember making the decision I was going to do more, be more and have more. I was good at school and followed the academic path like so many people do and followed what was suggested for me.

This is what I believed I had to do to create the life I wanted. This is what I was told by society to do.

I studied agricultural science at university and then went on to become a teacher and completed my Masters in Education. I married my husband and soon began the steep learning curve of running a family agricultural business and the long hours that went with it. Although the farm was making money and I was earning a wage, it felt like it was always a struggle. There was never enough money. And we never took time off. We became workaholics. We poured relentless hours into working physically but never really getting ahead. Not reaching the income that we desired.

I was doing what I had been conditioned to do. Get an education and work hard for your money. Now many people could be looking from the outside in thinking I had it all. The house, the land, a beautiful family. But there was something in me that just wasn't satisfied that this was it for the rest of my life. School gives you valuable knowledge but it doesn't teach you how to alter your subconscious programming, your paradigm.

I invested heavily into personal development. I really believed that I could be successful. And I wanted things to be different for my children. I had this inner desire that was growing.

But my self-image completely let me down. I didn't feel good enough, I continually compared myself to others. I didn't have confidence. I was scared of rejection. And I couldn't charge for my services. I wasn't aware about what was keeping me stuck. I felt like I was locked in a prison.

Now my problem became I wasn't earning the money that I truly wanted. I knew I was capable of doing it. I had the education, I was a hard worker and I put in the study. I felt I wasn't deserving of money and I didn't need much, just enough to survive. I had also learned that I had to work hard for my money. Not a fabulous recipe for the success I desired. Whatever I did didn't seem to be enough and there was something that I just wasn't getting.

It wasn't until I heard the phrase, "The more money you earn the more people you can help," that my whole perception around money changed. My strong desire has always been to help people get what they want. This change in perspective allowed me to create a healthier relationship with money and this began opening more doors for me to help more people – exponentially. And be paid for it.

I decided to focus on creating a millionaire self-image and realised that I had no idea what that looked and felt like.

If I didn't know what it was, I was sure there were plenty of other people out in the world wondering too.

Through this book it's my intention to help you create financial freedom in your life and pursue the things you've been justifying to yourself that you can't have.

I decided to interview other self-made millionaires to share their stories. This came literally as a flash idea in a conversation I was having. I took action immediately and the interviews were done and dusted in six weeks – and the result is some fabulous stories to share with you that will give you clarity and inspire you to take action for yourself.

How will you benefit from reading about this?

There are common themes that lead to the money and success that you desire. There will be one or two people that you resonate with and think – they're just like me. From others you'll take key parts and apply them to your life straight away.

In having greater awareness about this information, it's my intention that you will be able to do the following:

- Build the self-image that you desire for the person you want to become
- Create a healthy relationship with money that in turn will increase your income
- Create the life you truly want and understand anything is possible

What is expected of you?

Be open and willing to explore new information about the mind. Set your intentions. Complete the exercises throughout the book. Question yourself as you're going through the book, what are your beliefs? Each time you're asked a question, pause and THINK. I will continue to question you. I want you to really think, and I mean really think about what you are doing in your life. What do you really want to have? Then make the decisions you need for yourself to take you there. You'll be asked to re-read information. Repetition is the key to your understanding.

What is the best way to apply this?

As you read this book, I encourage you to use a pen/highlighter and underline points and parts that stand out for you. Read the book once in its entirety and then come back and read the book again and answer the questions. You'll find I will ask you questions throughout that get you to explore where you are presently and where you'd like to go. As you read through the book over and over, you'll come to understand the importance of repetition and increasing your awareness to get the results you truly want for your life.

Get yourself a notebook and answer the questions as you go. If you haven't done this before just do it. I did this myself with a book I read and have referred to my answers many times since. It's been a very enlightening process. Reflect and go back over each chapter. Underline, make notes, give yourself permission to write in the book and make it your own. Reflect, review, reflect, review. To get the most out of this book, you need to be really honest with yourself and apply the learning to your life. Study it daily. Set time aside each day where you can do this. You may find these requests and suggestions totally against what you would normally do. I want you to throw logic out the window. I want your mantra to be, "Do the illogical." The results will truly be worth it.

My Story

I started writing out an affirmation that "I have a millionaire self-image and it feels great." It got me really thinking. I wanted to become a self-made millionaire, I wanted more money. I wanted to achieve that to provide for my family – but where to start? I had never earned over 100k in a year. The most I'd ever earned was just under 90K, but I had the desire to earn so much more. I had earned this when I was a teacher. The wage was set. It wasn't dependent on how good a job I did or how committed I was. I could be the best teacher in the school and be paid the same as the worst teacher. This happens across the board. I was trading my time for money and I'd never really thought about it. I was also helping my husband build a multi-million dollar agricultural enterprise, but I didn't feel like that was my success. I wanted to do it for myself.

I'd been running a part-time business for three years and reached a good income level in the first five months but then didn't get any further. I was stuck. I was pouring time, money and effort into my business every day and not getting anywhere. I was thinking about it all the time and I couldn't switch off. I wasn't spending the time I wanted with my family. It seemed like it didn't matter how much action, I took I just couldn't move forward.

It wasn't until I heard the following sentence that I really questioned what I was earning. **The most important thing is understanding where you are:** I wasn't earning 90K because that's what I wanted to be earning. I was earning 90K a year because that's what I knew how to earn. I'm going to ask you to go back and read that sentence again because it's critical for you to understand and it's what's controlling the results in your life too.

Put your own income where mine is and read it out for yourself. Whether you are earning $36,000 a year, $100,000, $250,000, $500,000 a year, you're earning it because that's what you know how to do. It's what you're aware of what you're able to earn. It's not actually what you want, is it?

Do you know the difference between your mind and your intellect? I certainly didn't. You see I had grown up believing that to be successful in life you had to have a good education and work hard. So that's what I set out to do. I was an avid student and was focused on being successful. What I didn't know was that intellect/knowledge isn't everything. I had all these degrees on the wall but it didn't mean that I was going to be "successful."

Do you know people who are highly intelligent but broke? Do you know people who failed through school and are highly successful in business or their career? Me too. What I didn't know was that education wasn't enough. Intellect is just one part of the whole. There's the physical, the intellectual and the spiritual part of the body. I had focused on the physical and the intellect and found that it only got me so far. It wasn't until I heard the following story from Price Pritchett's book You2 that my whole world changed. It's a story about a fly who is buzzing at a window trying to get through the glass of the windowpane.

"The whining wings tell the poignant story of the fly's strategy – try harder. But it's not working. The struggle becomes part of the trap. It is impossible for the fly to try hard enough to succeed at breaking through the glass. Nevertheless, this little insect has staked its life on reaching its goal through raw effort and determination. This fly is doomed. It will die there on the windowsill. Across the room ten steps away, the door is open. Ten seconds of flying time and this small creature could reach the outside world. With only a fraction of effort being wasted, it could be free of this self-imposed trap. The breakthrough possibility is there. It would be so easy. Why doesn't the fly try another approach? How did it get so locked in on the idea that this particular route, and determined effort, offer the most promise for success? "Trying harder" isn't necessarily the solution to achieving more. It may not offer any real promise for getting what you want out of life. Sometimes, in fact, it's a big part of the problem. If you stake your hopes for a breakthrough on trying harder than ever, you may kill your chance for success."

I had a goal, though and was determined to achieve it. I have bucket loads of persistence and determination, and I was pouring time, money and effort into a business that wasn't moving forward. My husband was doing the same in his business. We could see what was possible for us, but we were that fly.

"If you find yourself in a hole, stop digging."
– Winston Churchill

What has this got to do with you? Everything. It's about your behaviour and what has been programmed in the subconscious part of your mind. That's what's showing up as results in your life.

You see I had learned growing up it was meant to be a struggle, to earn money was hard. You couldn't have what you wanted in life. You were supposed to be happy with what you got.

I was doing the same thing over and over and getting the same result. This is Albert Einstein's definition of insanity. And yes it was driving me crazy!

There had to be another way. And I was on the search. I was studying and reading personal development books everyday. I would move from one to the next voraciously looking for the answers.

What is a millionaire self-image? What does it look like? What does it feel like? How can I get one? What action do I need to take?

I actually had no idea.

I knew that I wanted that type of success and I was aware that I had to upgrade my self-image. Where to start? I knew people who were millionaires, but I saw them as no different than me and I couldn't understand why I couldn't become one too. What did I need to do?

Do you have that burning desire that you want to be more, do more and have more? You know you feel that you have way more to give, create and earn but you just don't know where to start?

Now one of the key things that we need to get you to understand is why you are where you are right now. You're not earning the income you have right now because that's what you want to earn. You are earning the income you have right now because that's what you know how to earn. This was a light bulb moment for me right here. Read that previous sentence over and over until you really understand what it means.

Ever had that feeling that your life was destined for success? That you want way more than what you have right now? That you want to be and do more than what you are currently doing? Guess what? You can have all that and more, but noone has taught you that it's possible. That's why you're where you are right now and I'm so pleased that you're reading this book because I know the information that you're going to receive will completely transform your thinking and your life, if you're committed to what you really want for your life.

What is success? When do you get there? Is it a destination?

My mentor Bob Proctor shared with me that his mentor defined success as the following: "Success is the progressive realization of a worthy goal." Now when you really think about this it's really incredible. It actually means that any person regularly engaging in achieving something which they consider worthy of themselves is successful. In other words, success happens along the way. It's the growth that you experience along the way to achieving your goal, not the final destination.

I also love what former First Lady Barbara Bush said about the future which you could certainly apply to success.

"We get on board that train at birth, and we want to cross the continent because we have in mind that somewhere out there is a station. We pass by sleepy little towns looking out the window of life's train, grain fields and silos,

level grade crossings, buses full of people on the roads beside us. We pass cities and factories, but we don't look at any of it because we want to get to the station. We believe that out there is a station where a band is playing and banners are hung and flags are waving and when we get there that will be life's destination. We don't really get to know anybody on the train. We pace up and down the aisles looking at our watches eager to get to the station because we know that life has a station for us.

This station changes for us during life. To begin with is that first promotion, and then the station becomes getting the kids out of college, and then the station becomes retirement and then... all too late we recognize the truth – that this side of that city whose builder is God, there really isn't a station. The joy is in the journey and the journey is the joy.

Sooner or later you realise that there is no station and the truth of life is the trip. Read a book, eat more ice cream, go barefoot more often, hug a child, go fishing, laugh more. The station will come soon enough. And as you go, find a way to make the world more beautiful."

With awareness and the right knowledge you can create your own millionaire self-image and live the life that you really want.

But what has the self-image of a millionaire got to do with it?

Quite frankly, absolutely everything. You can't outperform your self-image. The results in your life are a direct result of your self- image. How you see yourself.

Take responsibility for Yourself. You create your own reality – nobody else. If you aren't happy with the results in your life, you are the one that needs to change them. Now this can come across as harsh reality, but we have been taught to literally blame others for our circumstances, –"it's not my fault." When in reality your thoughts, feelings and actions underpin the results that are showing up in your life. If you don't like what's present – change it.

Look at where you are right now. What are the results for you in the following areas?

1) Health
2) Income
3) Relationships
4) Career

5) Finances

6) Holiday and travel

7) Community

8) Contribution

Are you happy with your results? Give yourself a rating out of 10 for each of these areas. What are you settling for? Are you even aware that you are settling? What are you justifying to yourself that you can't have?

Start looking at things with a different perspective. Problems will always be there. You have a choice to focus on the situation or focus on the solution. Those that are successful look at things in a different way, from a different perspective. Look at creating the life that you desire and actually go out there and start making it happen instead of waiting for the proof to show up in your life.

How it All Works

There are laws that govern nature. The same laws that govern the sun rising each day and an acorn seed planted in the ground growing into an oak tree. These same laws govern our thoughts and our mind. But we've never been taught what they are and how to use them. Until recently people thought that it was all alternate, new age stuff, and you don't want to know about that.

There is a science based around these laws and many people have been sharing this over the years. Dr Joe Dispenza, a neuroscientist and chiropractor, is squashing these myths. He's demonstrated the science behind the laws and your mind. He shares that everything in reality is vibrating in frequency and everything is energy. Thoughts have an electrical charge. Feelings have a magnetic charge. How you think and how you feel broadcasts an electromagnetic signal. Understanding this and applying this to your millionaire self-image is integral in ensuring your success. Your brain is a record of the past. It's a reflection of your environment. Your emotions stored in the body are also a record of past experiences.

Most people spend the majority of their time emotionally in the past and get emotionally involved with something that they can't change. When you begin to envision a possible future scenario, your brain has to work in different ways and you begin to construct a model you want to experience. As you begin to create this vision, the brain begins to freeze that picture inside and that's called intention. Intention is basically getting clear on what you want. You use your imagination to help you do this. When you start building that self-image of yourself as a millionaire, you'll create pictures, clear mental images. The thoughts that you want to have and the feelings you begin to feel will change everything – from energy to neurology, from chemistry to the genes, and the body.

It starts with the vision.

The vision we create in our mind in the future causes us to think and feel emotion. This can be positive or negative. You want to choose the positive, the picture of what you want.

Instead of using emotions to anchor us in the past like the majority of the population does, you have to learn how to think and feel your emotions in the future.

Dr. Joe Dispenza's work clearly backs this up with brain measurements and shows the changes in behaviour that occur, scientifically measured, with thoughts and the corresponding emotions.

The important thing here is to let go of the self-image you held of yourself in the past, and the thoughts and feelings linked to it. Your insecurities, self-doubt and lack of worth all need to be transformed into the emotional energy that you want in the future. You must live that feeling now. This becomes your compass your cybernetic instrument that guides you towards your goal.

PART ONE

CHAPTER 1 | PARADIGMS

*"This is really a black and white deal. It does not matter how
hard you work, or how many hours you put in.
If the paradigm does not change, ultimately the results will
remain much the same from one year to the next."*

– Bob Proctor

Two years ago, I had no idea what paradigms were. I had heard it used but I didn't really understand its application and the limitations that my paradigms were putting on my life and everyone around me. Finding out about paradigms was the biggest life-changing light bulb moment for me in my business and my life. I want to help you change the results in your life by sharing with you what paradigms are, how they may be limiting you and stopping you from having what you really want.

The **Oxford** *English Dictionary* defines the basic meaning of the term **paradigm** as "a typical example or pattern of something; a pattern or model." Bob Proctor defines a paradigm as "a mental program that has almost exclusive control over our habitual behaviour and almost all of our behaviour is habitual."

These habits are stored in our subconscious mind and passed on from generation to generation. They're also learned from our environment.

There are only two ways that you can change a paradigm. One is through constant spaced repetition and the other is through an emotional impact, which is usually from something negative. It could be a death in the family, loss of a job or, loss of a relationship.

Now one of the key things about paradigms is that paradigms are hard to change. You have to get the right direction and the awareness of what's limiting you. Once you get the right direction and understand how to change it, that's when your results will change. That is what I want to share with you in this book.

You need to understand where you are now, where you want to go and what paradigms are holding you back from getting there.

That's the key.

But you have to be serious about it. If you want to make the change you have to make a decision and really commit to yourself.

What do you want? I mean what do you really want? I spent most of my life focusing on all the things I didn't want. My paradigms were controlling what I thought was possible for my life. I continually compared myself to others and thought I wasn't good enough. I never measured up. I spent a lot of time and attention on what I didn't want. I want you to give yourself permission to start focusing on what you do want. What have you been telling yourself, justifying to yourself that you can't have?

Do you want to be earning more money? Do you want a new job, start a business, create multiple streams of income, have more time, more flexibility and freedom in your life to do the things that you want? It's all possible. However, we're not taught that it's possible. We're taught to settle and to be happy with what we have. Many of us have been conditioned to go without and are operating from a lack or limitation mindset.

I want you to take a look at your income for a moment. How much have you ever earned in your business/job in a year?

Why aren't you earning this each month? Take a moment and think about that.

The simple reason is that you have a paradigm around your relationship with money and a paradigm around your self-image. These two paradigms control your thoughts about what you think you're worth based on the beliefs that you've been programmed with. You've settled for what you have right now. And your logic can tell you that it's perfectly fine – that's just the way it's meant to be for you.

Your paradigms control everything. How you manage your business, your job, your money, your health, your relationships with your self, your partner, your family, your staff; it's all controlled by your paradigms.

Your paradigm controls your ability to earn money, your perception, your use of time, your creativity, your productivity and effectiveness and your logic. It's the limiting beliefs holding you back and you don't even know what they are. This is why so many people are stuck.

Why can some people be successful and others aren't? Why can a coffee shop go out of business and the same location reopens with a new coffee shop that becomes incredibly successful? This defies logic and the key is your paradigm. Our school systems concentrate on the logical/intellectual part of our mind. Now this only controls 5% of our behaviour. Meanwhile the subconscious part of our mind, our feeling part, controls 95% of our behaviour. We've been told that to be successful we need to get an education, to study and get a degree. But we've never been taught how our mind works, our paradigms or our conditioning.

Now let's consider this. Paradigms are other people's habits that have been passed from one generation to the next or what you were conditioned with environmentally growing up as a child. For many of you, your paradigm will be kicking in right now, switching off to what you're reading. Your inner thoughts will be telling you what I'm saying is total rubbish, and others of you will be reading this totally open to what I have written.

For some of you your paradigm will kick in after reading the book. You'll be inspired and want to find out more; and this too may pass. That is your paradigm holding you back. How many times have you got excited or inspired about something and then those thoughts kick in telling you, "I can go without, that isn't for me." That is the paradigm that's keeping you right where you are. The key is to become aware of this old conditioning and if it's not serving you, create a paradigm that does.

You'll recognize it and see other areas in your life where it's limiting you from moving forward. You squash your desire.

Your paradigms keep you where you are – in the comfort zone. If you want real changes in your business, your work and life, if you want to take control, you have to create a new paradigm.

I was a teacher for 15 years and have a few degrees: a Bachelors of Agricultural Science (Hons), Bachelor of Teaching, and a Masters of Education. I also have countless other pieces of paper showing you how much knowledge I have from other courses I've taken. Now I'm not sharing this with you to impress you, but to impress upon you that with all this education I'd been told to get to be successful, I just wasn't getting the results that I really desired. And I certainly wasn't happy. I was always striving to do the next course that would get me to where I wanted to go (or so I'd been conditioned to believe).

I was running my own business pouring lots of time, money and effort into it and not going anywhere and I couldn't understand why. My husband was also doing the same on the farm. Working ridiculously long hours, he was physically exhausted. Both of us working to create a life that our paradigms wouldn't allow. The money wasn't showing up, we didn't take holidays, we focused on the lack and limitation and all the things that were going wrong. I woke up one day completely and utterly frustrated, broke down in tears and threw my arms up in the air and shouted, "There has to be a better way!"

And then I learnt about paradigms and my life and my thinking changed, as did my results.

I had spent A LOT of time in my comfort zone. I told myself I couldn't catch up with friends or have holidays because I had to work. That we had to go without. All of this "self-talk rubbish" had really kept me from living!

I want to share this with you.

What is success? We have been taught to believe that it comes to someone who's highly educated. However, we all know people who have many degrees but aren't successful. And we all know people who have failed through school but have become successful entrepreneurs, don't we?

Your paradigms and the results that are showing in your life are what you have created. Now this is based on previous conditioning from previous generations as well as what you received in your environment growing up. You weren't responsible for putting the paradigms there, but you are responsible for changing them, if you want your results to change.

You can then make changes to design exactly what you want and create your own economy by building a new paradigm to replace the old, and close what we call "the knowing/doing gap." To create permanent change, we must change the primary cause – the paradigm.

> *"To the question of your life, you are the only answer.*
> *To the problems of your life, you are the only solution."*
> – **Jo Coudert (Author)**

The real cause behind the results in your life is your thinking. To change the results in your life, your thinking has to change and you have to take personal responsibility for your productivity.

Imagine yourself jumping out of bed each morning inspired about the day ahead, working towards your goal and what you love to do.

If you're willing and want to change your paradigm, it's never about what's happening outside of you. It's always about what happens on the inside. It's actually all about your thinking. For you to get that millionaire self-image and money in the bank, you've got to change your thinking. So how do you do that?

Let's take a look at your mind. Do you know what it is? When you think of your mind, most of us automatically think of our brain. The truth is that no one has ever seen the mind.

Let me give you an example.

I want you to picture yourself walking up to your front door. Just take a moment and look at your front door. Look down at the door handle. I want you to be conscious of which way you have to turn or move the handle to open the door. What does it feel like? Is it warm or cold to the touch? I want you to walk in through your door through to your kitchen, being aware of the noise that your feet are making as you walk. I want you to go to your refrigerator and stand in front of it. What colour is it? What photos or things are stuck on it or is it bare? I want you to open the door, thinking about which way it opens. On the top shelf is a plate of lemons that have been cut up into wedges. I want you to reach out and grab one feeling the coolness of it. I want you to smell the lemon before you take a big bite into it.

You have just experienced a range of senses from feeling the door, hearing your shoes on your floor as you walked, smelling and tasting the lemon. You may have had a physical response to this and salivated when you thought about biting into the lemon. Your mind is in every cell of your body. Mind is what controls your body. It controls the movement of your body. It controls what you experience. You didn't physically get up and leave the room and go to your house, you were able to do this in your mind. And your mind is a tool that we haven't been taught how to use. It's important to understand it, so that you understand the hold that the paradigm has and how to change it.

We have two parts to our mind. The conscious and the subconscious.

The Conscious Mind

We have our conscious mind where we take in and gather information through our five senses by what we see, hear, taste, touch, and smell. This part of the mind stores information from the experiences and knowledge we've gained. It is the "knowing" part of the mind. As you are reading this book, you are gathering information. The conscious mind is also the part of the mind that we do our thinking from. Thoughts and ideas go in and out of your conscious mind. It's where ideas originate. Here, you create your wants and desires.

The Subconscious Mind

The second part to your mind is the subconscious mind. It's the part of the mind that controls your actions or simply put, the "doing" part of the mind. What controls your actions? Your behaviour controls your actions. And your habits control your behaviours. Your subconscious mind is in control of what you do and how well you do it.

The subconscious mind needs to be changed to create better results. The things you're doing right now, you've been programmed to do. You don't even know why you do some of the things you do. And this is where your paradigm is stored it's stored in a section of your subconscious mind.

For you to increase your income and create your new way of living, you'll need to study this. You'll want to know how you are programmed.

What are some things that you are doing that continue to get in your way?

Thinking is the highest function we are capable of, and yet most people don't think. They think they think, but they don't. Mental activity doesn't constitute thinking. If you pay close attention to what people are saying or doing, you'll soon see that they're not thinking, otherwise, they'd never be doing what they do.

A person would never intentionally do something that resulted in a negative outcome. What happens is the paradigm takes over the thinking. And you must become aware of this. When you're aware of the thoughts that you're thinking, you can make the choice to choose thoughts that are going to give you the results you actually want.

Now this is critical for you to understand. Your thoughts create feelings, your feelings cause you to take action and then you get your results. If you don't like the results the only way you can change them is by going back to the source, your thoughts. Are they in alignment with what you desire?

This is where the knowing/doing gap comes in and it's truly powerful because you can change anything by creating an awareness around what's actually happening and then implement one or two habits to take a different action towards your goal, closing the gap.

Our paradigms tend to keep us focused in the past and emotionally connected with things that have happened that we can't change or control. We can use our mind in exactly the same way to move us forward into the future and focus on the things that we really want.

SUMMARY

- A paradigm is a mental program that has almost exclusive control over our habitual behaviour and almost all of our behaviour is habitual
- There are two ways that you can change a paradigm: through repetition or an emotional impact
- Education alone is not enough. You must take action.
- You can change your paradigm by choosing the thoughts, feelings and actions that are in alignment with the results that you want

CHAPTER 2 | ATTITUDE

*"Attitude is the reflection of a person and
the world mirrors our attitude."*

– Earl Nightingale

There's a reason Earl Nightingale said attitude really is the magic word. The key to your success in everything is wrapped up in this package. Your attitude towards yourself, your attitude towards others, your attitude towards money; your relationships; your success; your environment.

But what really is an attitude?

Googling attitude you can find a definition like this:

*"a settled way of thinking or feeling about someone or something,
typically one that is reflected in a person's behaviour."*

Earl Nightingale described attitude as

"a composite of your thoughts, your feelings and your actions."

Growing up as a child and going through school, you were told to have a good attitude. I always took it to mean I had to behave a certain way. If you don't understand attitude, then how can you improve it? It wasn't until I started really studying attitude in depth that things started to change for me. Give this chapter serious attention – it can change your results faster and more dramatically than anything else. In fact, William James said the greatest discovery of his generation was that you could alter your life by altering your attitude of mind.

Really think about where your attitude is set right now. You can have an outward positive attitude but still have a negative mindset. This doesn't mean that you're a negative person. It means that whenever you're operating from a place of lack or limitation you're operating with a negative attitude. While you have one thing in your mind you have another thing happening physically and the results you desire won't show up for you. When you express yourself, you can be coming from past, present, future. You want to train your attitude to focus on the future where you want to be, an expression of the good that you desire.

Three Parts of Your Attitude

There are three parts to your attitude – thoughts, feelings and actions. Your attitude is a composition of these three things. Now this is critical to understand. It's not just one thing; it's all of these parts that make up your attitude. It's a bit like making a cake. You don't make a comment that its great flour or great eggs, you comment on the whole cake and say it's a great cake. To change and improve your attitude you really have to explore and understand those three ingredients – thoughts, feelings and actions.

You can do this for all areas in your life but let's get you started with your attitude, specifically around money. If you're paying attention, you'll notice I'm always getting you to start where you are right now. That's because it's part of the problem of why you are where you are. Each activity I'm walking you through is growing your awareness and this will allow your future money attitude to develop.

What is your attitude towards money like right now? Is money flowing to you abundantly (10/10) or are you finding that you never have enough (4/10). Give yourself a rating out of 10 as to what this is for you. Then what we are going to doing is take each part of your attitude and brainstorm all of what makes up the whole.

What are your thoughts around money?

What are your feelings around money?

What are your actions around money?

Really take some time to write this all down. It's really important to get it down on paper or type it out because this causes you to think. Divide a page into three and write the headings thoughts, feelings and actions. And as you are doing this you may find thoughts that you weren't even aware of that are hidden your subconscious. This is such a brilliant exercise to do.

Once you've done that reflect and revise your answers.

Did you have **thoughts** like:

- Money is hard to get
- You've got to work hard to get money
- Only the rich can earn money
- I never have enough money
- Money comes to me easily
- I find it easy to make money
- I know where the money is

Did you have **feelings** of:

- Fear
- Frustration
- Worry
- Excitement
- Anger
- Abundance

What **actions** are you taking in your life around money?

- Are you disciplined with your money?
- Do you save your money, do you spend it?
- Do you spend it on yourself?
- Are you always looking for what's on special?
- Do you select the cheapest thing on a menu or have what you want?
- Do you fight with your partner over money?

Whatever it is for you just get it out of that mind of yours. Get it on paper so you can really see what is buried in your mind.

Think about your relationship with money. Realise what you have in front of you has been your attitude towards money and it has acted like a control mechanism programmed to the attitude that you had towards it. If you want your results to change, then you have to change your attitude.

Now I want you to imagine yourself as a millionaire. Let's have a look at what your attitude towards money would be now.

What thoughts do you think you would be having about money?

What feelings do you think you would be having around money? What actions would you be taking with your money?

This will really cause you to think. How would a millionaire think, feel and act? You've got to get inside their heads. Would you be worried about how much money was in your bank account? Would you be concerned about the price of groceries at the supermarket? Would you be worried about having enough money for petrol, going on a holiday, buying a piece of clothing that you wanted?

No, you'd possibly be having thoughts like, "It's easy to create money." "It's fun to create all I desire and I always have the money to do what I want." or "Money comes to me easily."

Having evaluated the attitude of a millionaire, these are the thoughts, feelings and actions that you need to be upgrading as your attitude towards money. You need to make these attitudes the ones you hold in mine and change your old programming to bring in the new. Creating this new, millionaire attitude will cause different results in your life – results that you desire.

"We must be the epitome, embodiment of success.
We must radiate success before it will come to us.
We must first become mentally, from an attitude standpoint,
the people we wish to become."

– Earl Nightingale

Your attitude is a choice. Until now you probably haven't even been aware of many of the thoughts, feelings and actions that have been programmed into you, particularly about your money paradigm.

Remember, some of your current attitude is the composite of another person's set of beliefs and habits that were passed on to you. Many successful people have had a healthy attitude and belief system around money and that's why they are so successful. Others made decisions to change their existing programming and at many times were unaware that they had done this. You are now going to be aware of what you need to change here and realise that you can change your paradigm.

The goal is to have your thoughts, feelings and actions in alignment with your new money paradigm. It won't serve you to upgrade your actions around money and start spending it, if you haven't changed your thoughts and feelings. The key is alignment. When you do this, your attitude will become the catalyst for change.

I felt a huge shift in myself physically and my awareness took a quantum leap when I did this simple exercise. I was taking massive action in my business, but my thoughts were negative and my feelings flat and despondent. I had a positive outlook, but a negative mindset. I was coming from a place of lack and limitation. Upon realizing this, I looked at the thoughts that I needed to have to achieve the results I desired. I then started to apply the exercise and think these thoughts and become aware of the feelings I desired to have and change them.

I had a client who realised when doing this activity that she had the thoughts and feelings but there was no action.

Situation/Solution Exercise

I do this exercise regularly.

Whenever I have a problem, I write it at the top of a page and write the word "Situation." I then do the inventory of my existing thoughts, feelings and actions.

I turn the page over and then write at the top "Solution" – the outcome I desire. I write out the thoughts, feelings and actions that I need to have to achieve the results. This creates the right attitude and the right feeling to "attract" those results. Whatever is in alignment with the feeling that you are having is what you are going to attract. Just like a magnet.

Be a Money Magnet

Neville Goddard, author of "The Power of Awareness" says, "*The rich man, poor man, beggar man and thief are not different minds but just different arrangements of the same mind. Just like a piece of steel when magnetized differs not in substance from its demagnetized state, but in the arrangement and order of its molecule.*" When a piece of steel or anything else is demagnetized, the magnetism, has not gone out of existence. There is only a rearrangement of the particles, so that they produce no outside or perceptible effect. When particles are arranged at random, mixed up in all directions, the substance is said to be demagnetized. When the particles all face in one direction the substance is a magnet.*"

In Absence of Magnetic Field   In Presence of Magnetic Field

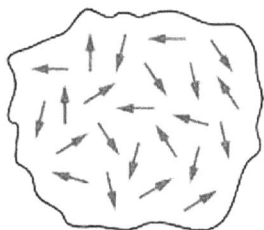

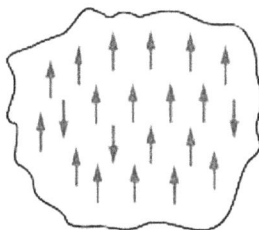

How does this apply to attitude? Remember your attitude is a composite of your thoughts, feelings and actions. When these are in alignment, you create a magnet for all the good that you desire. When they're not in alignment, you become demagnetized to the good and attract whatever you're in harmony with. Your results = your attitude. Change your attitude = Change your results.

This is also true for your goals. Your thoughts are like your Global Positioning System (GPS). What is your internal GPS set to? Even if you have a goal – if your thoughts, actions and feelings are like the picture on the left – all over the place – you'll be driving around aimlessly in your life.

When you have an understanding that your thoughts, feelings and actions need to be in alignment with your goal, you'll create clarity and focus. Where you're going will be like the picture on the right and everything will move forward.

Do an inventory for yourself.

1. Do you have a clear goal that you are emotionally connected with?
2. How is your attitude? Are your thoughts feelings and actions in alignment?
3. What are you being guided to?

We tend to settle for what's easy and miss the abundance and satisfaction that's right here waiting for us to become aware.

Listen and say yes to opportunities that are coming your way, be it people, resources, invitations or offers.

What can you say YES to that will make a change for you moving forward?

The key for you now is to think, feel and act like a millionaire. Be the person that you want to become and imagine yourself right into the feeling of being that person with all that you desire.

This attitude goes out into all areas of your life.

Whenever you have a problem in your relationships, health, job, business etc., I suggest doing this same exercise and unpack your thoughts feelings and actions. Become aware and then transform the thoughts, feelings and actions into the attitude necessary to get the result you desire.

As I was writing this chapter of the book, I had a break and flicked through my Facebook stream to find a snippet of a video on Roger Federer and the transformation that occurred for him as a tennis player.

He had the desire to be the best tennis player in the world from a young age. His temperament got in the way of his success. He had a poor attitude. His coach saw incredible potential in him but realised his attitude was not serving him, so he set about teaching Roger to be polite and gracious. The key here was that Roger couldn't be told, he had to make the decision to change for himself and he did.

"You will not grow if you are not willing to change yourself"
– Roger Federer

You have the potential to grow into the person that you truly want to become, but you have to make the decision to do so.

Attitude of Gratitude

This is the right place to share about an attitude of gratitude. In "The Science of Getting Rich," Wallace Wattles tells us, *"The whole process of mental adjustment and attunement (letting go) can be summed up in one word: "gratitude."*

An attitude of gratitude can transform how you are feeling in an instant and you don't need money to do it – it's completely free! The key is to feel good. When you become aware that your attitude isn't serving you, perhaps your thoughts or feelings are out of alignment. Shift to finding something you're grateful for and you can change your feelings and your corresponding attitude in an instant.

We'll talk more about gratitude when we discuss daily habits for success in Part 3 of this book.

Fundamentals of Attitude

I expect good things to happen to me every day.

I plant as many 'good thought' seeds as I can every day so I **know** those seeds have to come to fruition. I always expect good things to happen and when something happens that seems, to others, to have pushed me off-track, I look for the good in the event, because I know it has to be there.

Good, bad, up, down; inside, outside; big, small; everything has its opposite. The law of polarity dictates that. Where there are problems, there are always opportunities. You just need to stop and think and then look for them. Simply by placing your attention there you will expand it and draw the opportunity toward you.

There was once a time when I didn't expect good things and therefore didn't receive them. Now I receive great things.

I surround myself with great people and watch them do amazing things. I learn from them, see the good that they do and wish even greater things for them. An expectant mind leads to an attitude of gratitude.

Expect the best for you, your family, your business and your community.

Positive Attitude Exercise

Here are positive statements I read regularly to improve my attitude.

Choose 30, 60 or 90 days where you read these statements and think about how they apply to your goal and your life right now.

"A great attitude becomes a great mood, which becomes a great day, which becomes a great year, which becomes a great life."
– Zig Ziglar

*"A bad attitude is like a flat tyre –
you can't go anywhere until you change it."*
– Anonymous

"Our environment is really a mirror of our mental attitude. If we don't like our environment, we have to change our attitude first."
– Earl Nightingale

SUMMARY

- Attitude is a composite of your thoughts, feelings and actions
- You can have a positive outward attitude but have a negative mindset
- Your attitude is like a magnet – it attracts whatever you're in harmony with
- You can change your attitude
- Choose your thoughts, feelings and actions so that they are in alignment with the results that you desire.

CHAPTER 3 | AWARENESS

*"What is necessary to change a person, is to
change his awareness of himself"*
– Abraham Maslow

I was aware that I wanted more for my life and I felt locked in a prison but it wasn't until I became aware that I had a choice, that it was my responsibility to make the changes for myself, that things began to change. That's what I want for you as well.

What is awareness? Great question when you start to dig a little bit deeper and become aware – quite literally!

Google definition is as follows

"knowledge or perception of a situation or fact."

Understanding awareness was a completely new concept to me. Like paradigms, it's a word that changed my life for the better.

You see, I had the belief that to be successful in life I had to have an excellent education. I set out to achieve that. I got excellent grades at school, earned three degrees at University and completed countless other courses and programs. But my results indicated that I wasn't successful in the way that I wanted to be successful. I was successful in many areas: a happy marriage four beautiful children, and financially I was doing okay. But there was something inside of me that wanted more. I was completely dissatisfied with my results and couldn't understand why I hadn't achieved the way I wanted to. I had this desire to be and do more. It wasn't until I became aware of paradigms that my whole perception changed. My growing awareness and understanding led me to writing this book and sharing this information with you so that your awareness changes and you see what is truly possible for you in your life.

When you were born, you had a heightened level of awareness. You had to become aware of the differences between male and female, you had to become aware of how to crawl, to walk, to talk, to play, to ride a bike and do all the amazing things you did as a child. Then when you started school, the focus was turned to your intellect and the awareness side of you was used less and less until it became barely used at all.

You became focused on learning information, which was directed by your teachers, and you become less and less aware. You received a report at school which graded you on your ability to retain knowledge. And for most people this was where their self-image came from – how good they were at remembering knowledge. You also measured how well you did to other members of your class and graded yourself in your mind. If you didn't remember the knowledge, then you received a report that gave you a low grade. This meant you weren't smart. Does this sound familiar to you?

This is the program we've all been fed. To be a success you have to be good at school. It's just not true. It's a complete and utter lie. You know plenty of people who've failed school and become incredibly successful multi-million-dollar entrepreneurs.

Their success wasn't dependent on their report card. Too often though, your self-image is shaped by this and you "believe" what's possible for you based on these results or what other people tell you you're capable of. The common formula became poor report card = "I'm not good enough," "I'm not smart enough," and people give up because they lack belief about what's really possible for them.

You weren't graded on your ability or your potential or awareness of your surroundings, just the knowledge that you retained at one moment in time. And this knowledge may be something that doesn't even interest you. You may have extensive knowledge and interest in an area, but you have to do what everyone else is doing in the curriculum to fit the system. This says nothing about the infinite potential within you.

When you start to really think about this it doesn't make much sense. I remember having to rote learn the entire animal classification table for an exam for Zoology. I questioned myself then – what's the point of this? Then when I became a teacher, I did exactly the same thing to my students. Now in some schools there are some changes occurring, but for the majority this process is still the norm.

Your level of awareness of yourself is actually the measurement of your success, not the amount of knowledge you can retain and repeat back.

I shared earlier that if you were earning 30K, 50K 100K or 250K a year this was because this was what you were aware that you could earn.

I want you to really understand that it's actually because you are not aware of how to earn more. You have been programmed in your subconscious mind to earn a set amount of money, regardless of what you do or whether or not it's what you want to earn. You may want to earn a million dollars, but you're not aware of how to do this.

Let's delve deeper into awareness and what it means for you.

There are seven levels of awareness as described by Earl Nightingale in his "Lead the Field" program. I want you to take a look at them and choose the level that you are on presently, where you think you are right now.

7. Mastery

6. Experience

5. Discipline

4. Individual

3. Aspiration

2. Mass

1. Animal

Animal is the first level, it's fight or flight and this is where a person is in reactionary mode. The next level is mass consciousness. It's where the individual stays and follows whatever the crowd does. This is where most people are and stay. Ask yourself what course am I following? Am I following people that will get me to where I want to go? Do I aspire to be and have more?

When I studied this program, aspiration stood out to me. This is where I was for a large part of my life. I spent much of my time frustrated. I lacked awareness about my paradigms and the limitations that were stopping me from moving forward. I had started to move away from the mass and be courageous to explore the drive inside me. The desire to be more, have more and do more was driving me. Where you aspire to be more than who you are there is this constant searching for doing or wanting something better. This is a good thing. When you understand that your spirit (the bit that makes you, you) is for continual expansion and expression, you can understand this is where the desire for more comes from.

When this happens you may step away from the mass or you may stay where you are. What do you need to move from mass to aspiration? The desire. You've been programmed to conform, to be like everyone else. This is what's keeping you where you are right now. What keeps you in the mass? It's feelings of judgment and rejection from others when you step away from the pack. You have to overcome the fear of moving away from the pack to step into your greatness.

"The opposite to courage in our society is not cowardice, it is conformity."
– Rollo May.

I absolutely love this quote and it's at the forefront of my mind in my own journey. Look at your life right now. What are you conforming to? Who do you follow? Who are you in alignment with? Think of your house, your clothes, the car you drive, holidays and where you go; the people you spend the most of your time with. Are these things that you want? And I mean really want. Are you **aware** of what you're actually conforming to? Have you ever consciously asked yourself? Is this what I want? What are you compromising?

Abraham Maslow said, "You'll either step forward into growth or backwards into safety." When you go forward into growth it can be scary. It's what you need to do. Otherwise you will stay stuck in your comfort zone, and just exist.

If you have that desire you'll have to move away from the mass conformity that your life has been in alignment with.

Remember you are the sum of the five people you spend the most time with. This blew me away when I first heard it. The more success/personal development books you read, you'll find this is a common thread throughout.

Who are the five people you spend your time with and how do they influence the decisions you make in your own life?

Are you **aware** of your decisions?

Are you even making your own decisions?

If you don't have the desire, then we'll have to work on that in the coming chapter on **goals**.

Awareness is the key to taking the first step. The next step is to be courageous. What is it that you really want? You're reading this book because you want more. More freedom, more money, more satisfaction, more success in any area of your life.

If it's the money you desire it's more about what the money can actually provide for you. It's freedom, more choices, time to live your life the way you really want to.

If you've spent most of your life conforming to the masses, you've probably been telling yourself you want to be a millionaire. In the next thought, you tell yourself that's not possible, it's not for you. Well I'm here to tell you it is, and you've been lying to yourself for years.

It is time to become aware of your thoughts because you can have what you want. You can have more money and live your life the way you really want to. Just make a decision.

Combine getting outside your comfort zone, a clearly defined goal and the desire to do it and you are well on your way.

You'll need to make some changes and that's why the majority of people stay earning their 30K, 50K, 100K or 250K a year because they aren't prepared to do the work on themselves, get uncomfortable and do whatever it takes.

You'll face terror barriers over and over, but that's where the growth really is. It's getting uncomfortable and going against the mass conformity that stops people in their tracks. You'll experience discomfort, you'll experience rejection, you'll question yourself. But it's worth it. This is part of your life, your journey to becoming the person you really want to be. And this is your growing awareness about yourself.

Once you've sorted out your aspirations, then you move into the next step – **individual**. This is all about you. This is where your talents, your gifts, your potential, everything that makes you unique lies. All the stuff you've probably been hiding in the past is about to see the light of day. This is where you get to express your uniqueness as a human being and do what you love, what you really love and are good at. Every single person is good at something that no-one else can do, that's what makes us an individual. Becoming aware of this will require you to be open, direct and be really honest with yourself about who you really are, your unique talents and abilities.

This is going to take **discipline**. This is the step that can trip up a lot of people because of all the limiting beliefs that have been programmed into you. These beliefs stop you from achieving and doing the things that you've been designed to do in your lifetime. You see, discipline is a word that was associated with punishment for a lot of us growing up. Instead, Bob Proctor defines discipline as "*the ability to give yourself a command and follow it.*" This is a productive habit that you'll need to develop in all areas of your life. Take a look and see where you're unable to be disciplined. You'll need to create a new habit and continue to practice and practice this until you've mastered it.

Most people give up. They don't understand it's not their habit they've been battling with and it's time to dig deep and start changing. It's a mental muscle that really needs a good work out. I know this was an area where I really lacked. On the outside people saw me as disciplined. Internally this wasn't the case. It wasn't until I started doing a course that said you had to master the discipline of a daily and weekly routine that I realised it didn't matter how much knowledge I had. If I couldn't put it into the action I needed to take, I wasn't going to move any further ahead in my life. The same goes for you. To move to the next level, you have to build your discipline muscle until you can give yourself that command and follow it. You'll surprise yourself at how productive you become as well.

Gaining discipline will allow you to move on to the next level of awareness – **experience**. This is where all your learning actually comes into play. Throughout school you were focused on gathering of information and repeating it back to your teacher/lecturer. You may or may not have become emotionally involved with what you were doing. However, with this level of awareness you're actually focused on consciously entertaining the learning. You get emotionally involved with it and actually step out and take action. You experience it and apply it to what you're doing and you change the result. It's all about taking action. This is where the growth comes in. The conscious experience of this change causes your behaviour to change and therefore your results to change as a result of this action. This is what learning is all about.

And when you experience this, it moves you into the final level of awareness, which is **mastery**. This is where you've implemented your potential, your ideas, been disciplined and taken action over and over until you've mastered it and it's become part of who you are. This is the process that takes you to raising your level of income to where you desire it to be. It's not more information/knowledge, it's your growing awareness that's going to take you there. At present if you changed this awareness even 1% in your life right now, the results would be phenomenal.

Now that you're aware of that lets move into goals and making sure that you have the right ones to get you to where you really want to go.

SUMMARY

- Your level of awareness of yourself is actually the measurement of your success
- There are seven levels of awareness:
    - i. Animal
    - ii. Mass
    - iii. Aspiration
    - iv. Individual
    - v. Discipline
    - vi. Experience
    - vii. Mastery
- Step into growth and be courageous
- Goals, desire, decision and discipline are intertwined with growing your awareness

CHAPTER 4 | GOALS

*"In absence of clearly defined goals we become strangely loyal to
daily trivia and ultimately we become enslaved by it."*

– Robert Heinlein

I've always been a goal setter. I've been a religious setter of SMART
(Specific, Measurable, Attainable, Realistic, Time-based) goals, always
achieving and ticking off my list, every year. Each year I'd write my goals
for the new year and at the end of the year tick off all that I had achieved.

It wasn't until I heard goals defined in a different way that I realised
why I wasn't happy with all that I was achieving. I just wasn't emotionally
connected with my goals. Don't get me wrong, I was highly productive and
have done some amazing things, but a lot of these goals were going in the
opposite direction of what I actually wanted. I had goals I thought I wanted
to achieve based on my belief systems, how I had been brought up and
what I "thought" I should be doing with my life. These weren't truly what I
wanted for my life. Does that make sense?

What I know for sure is that you have to set the right type of goal that's
in harmony with what you want, so that you think about and feel your goal
every day. It inspires you, motivates you and is something that you truly
want for yourself, for your life.

Clearly defined goals create a greater sense of wellness in a person because
the picture of the goal brings the mind and body into an orderly state.
Where there is no order in the mind, disorder and confusion set in, which
can lead to feelings of worry, fear, anxiety and a body that's not at ease. The

true purpose of a goal is actually to help you grow spiritually, mentally, emotionally and physically. You'll become addicted to feelings of inspiration and desire as you move towards goals you really want.

Setting the Right Type of Goal

Most of us have been taught to set SMART goals (specific, measurable, attainable, realistic, timely). But the problem with these goals is that they quite often lack inspiration and people give up on them or achieve them like I did with no emotional connection.

There are three types of goals according to Bob Proctor, my mentor, who has been studying the human mind, potential and growth in business for the past 57 years. You'll hear his story in an upcoming chapter. They are the ABCs' of goal setting.

Type A goals – present results. Something you already know how to do. This could be going on a holiday or buying a car. If you've done this before it's not a real goal, as you already know how to do it and it's not going to make you grow. If you haven't done something before that's a great goal to set if you really want it.

Type B goals – These goals are what you think you can do. If all of these things happen, you've done your research, you have a plan in place, you know you can accomplish this goal. There's no inspiration here. People quite often get bored, quit and give up. This usually pertains to SMART goals.

Type C goals – Now this is the type of goal you really want to be setting. Ask yourself what do I really want? Most people don't know what they really want, so you need to spend some time doing this. And if you know how to reach it, it's the wrong goal. You need to imagine and fantasize here.

The key is that you don't have to know how to do it. The fun is finding out how you're going to do it. Those of you who are logically programmed and have spent most of your life in your left-brain are going to have to branch out into that right side of your brain, and start thinking creatively. And if you're a logical thinker, you may have a difficult time with this concept. You learned in the chapter on paradigms that you have to start thinking illogically. Start now and override your paradigm.

We have been conditioned as school children to be limited in our dreaming or use of our imagination. We think we're meant to know how things happen, we're taught to be logical. However, Type C goals come from your fantasies and are originated through effective use of your imagination. This really is an area of our brain that many of us no longer know how to use. I certainly found this difficult to begin with but it does get easier as you focus on it, think about it and mix it with feelings. The indicator for me is this goal will both scare and excite you at the same time. This is the feeling that you want to experience for your Type C goal and that's confirmation you're on the right track.

With that in mind think about what you really want. Spend some time doing this. Then write a list of all the things that you want. I found this a very difficult exercise to begin with, but I encourage you to persist with it. It was challenging because I had always focused on what I didn't want. The key is to start writing and activating your thinking mind. Keep asking yourself over and over, what do I really want, what do I really want? What ideas have you thought of and rejected? What things do you tell yourself you can't do? What is something you've thought of doing but told yourself it would be impossible, cost too much, or you're not good enough?

I had a breakthrough when I was asked, "What have you been justifying to yourself that you have to go without?" Flip it and you will find a list of wants right there. What's a goal that excites and scares you at the same time that you've never accomplished but would love to do? It doesn't matter what age you are; your goals are there to help you grow.

A goal achiever becomes a productive person. They frequently accomplish more in one year than most individuals do in an entire lifetime. And it's all a choice.

Research studies have shown that by setting your goals out and writing them down, you have more chance of actually achieving them.

Take some time now and make a list of all the things you want. Totally relax and let your imagination wander. You're capable of doing anything. Use these phrases to start you off, "It would be so amazing if…" "I would love to … "I've always dreamed of doing…"

I suggest that you take some time over the next couple of days and weeks and continually add to your list. By creating this list, you're raising your conscious awareness. When you decide on the one thing on the list that you want more than anything else, that becomes the star you're shooting for. That becomes your type C goal. When you do what you love, you'll never work another day in your life. This is the feeling of freedom you want to feel when you're setting your goal, keeping in mind that millionaire self-image you're developing.

This really gets you thinking about what you really want – is it more time, more freedom, more money, a change in career? What's actually possible? And really the answer is anything your mind can think of. Sounds crazy right? But we all have infinite potential we haven't tapped into. We only use 5-10 % of our mind and many of us are going through the motions of life. Not really excited about our day ahead.

How many people are getting up and going to a job they don't enjoy every day? Hitting the snooze button over and over, and really not living a life that they love? I'm guessing millions and millions.

Understand that you actually have a choice. You might not think that right now with your current conditioning, but you truly do. You have created everything in your life, possibly without even thinking about it. This book is all about getting you to really think about your life, create your millionaire self-image so you can get out there and really live the life you truly want.

Look at what was achieved from the invention of the airplane to landing on the moon in the space of 66 years. The same creative state should and can be entered by anyone and enjoyed every day of your life. This happens when you set type C goals. It's not about being smart. There are plenty of people out there who have minimal education that have become very successful entrepreneurs. You know some yourself. It's is connecting your desire with a goal that you want, but have no idea how you'll achieve it.

When thinking of your goals compare them to Edmund Hilary climbing Mount Everest. Understand there are steps you need to take to get you to where you want to go. And sometimes the whole staircase won't be in full view. You'll have to take sidesteps and go back down a couple of steps. But, you may also have quantum leaps and jump five steps at once. Understand that focusing on your goal, constantly thinking about it and taking action is the key.

Also, understand that sometimes the plan changes. It's a type C goal, you won't know how you're going to get there. Edmund Hilary had failed attempts. He had to get to a number of base camps before he got to the top. You'll find that you'll have action steps along the way that lead you to your type C goal.

Most of us spend so much time focusing on lack and all our limitations and what we haven't achieved that we neglect to celebrate all the things we have done. Writing a list of wins each week will give you a sense of accomplishment. An effective goal will inspire you and make you grow.

I'm not saying I've achieved every goal I've set for myself. I certainly haven't. I continually revisit my goals and know that each step allows me to grow as a person. It's always important to reflect as well to see what you've achieved and how much you've grown.

Think about that for yourself. What have you achieved? What are your wins? What have you done well? Where can you improve or fine tune? Start training yourself to focus on all the good, all the wins and what you really want. As you do this, you'll notice a change as your focus changes.

How the mind works

"Nothing is impossible to the mind.
All its guidance and power is available to you when
you fully realise thoughts cause all.
You will know that there will never be any limits
that you yourself do not impose."
– U.S. Anderson

This will really help you understand goal setting and how to make best use of it. If I ask you to bring up an image of a lemon, your front door or your kitchen, what do you see? You can easily bring up these pictures in your mind. But if I ask you to bring up an image of your mind – nothing - right? No-one has ever seen the mind before. The mind thinks in pictures which is why a vision board is great, but I'll cover that at another time.

"You must imagine yourself
right into the state of the fulfilled desire."
– Neville Goddard

Imagination is the key and yet it's not something that's taught in schools. It's actually switched off in many of us. Knowledge is concentrated in the conscious part of the mind. The imagination is one of our intellectual faculties. Imagination is where all good ideas, inventions and success have originated, from the light globe to the car, to the technology that we have in our phones.

What is the mind? Dr. Thurman Fleet in San Antonio, Texas was very involved in the healing arts. Dr. Fleet realised that he and others in his profession were treating the symptoms and not the cause of the problems. He had said that when it came to the mind that there was confusion and he created a picture of the mind to help people understand – The mind functions on two levels and is divided into two parts

WHAT IS THE MIND?

Dr. Thurman Fleet – 1934

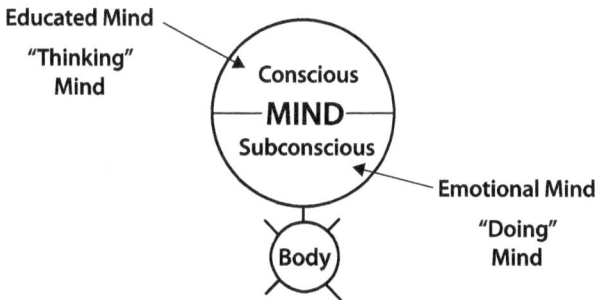

1) The conscious mind (thinking mind) relies on your five senses – sight, taste, touch, hearing and smell. We can choose our thoughts here because our conscious mind can choose to accept or reject ideas.

2) The subconscious mind (emotional/feeling mind).
   The subconscious mind is your power central – it functions in every cell of your body. This is the part of the mind where we store our memories, habits, conditioned beliefs and self-image. Our subconscious mind can't tell the difference between positive or negative results. It will do whatever we tell it.

When we originate thoughts in our conscious mind (setting goals) and impress them on our subconscious mind by becoming emotionally involved with these thoughts, this causes feelings, which then causes you to take actions which causes results.

This is why it is so important to choose your thoughts. Understanding this means that we can choose to focus on what we want rather than what we don't want. Because what we think about comes about. And choosing the thoughts we truly want to have is the hardest thing that you can possibly do.

"There is no labor from which most people shrink as they do from that of sustained and consecutive thought; it is the hardest work in the world."

– Wallace Wattles

What holds you back from achieving your goals?

The two most important things to understand are where you are right now and where you want to go. The where you want to go is where most people focus their attention. They set goals and have a destination, but quite often don't achieve these goals and spend plenty of time frustrated, confused and berating themselves. Why does success come easily for some people while for others it appears that it doesn't matter what they do, they always fall short of the mark?

It has to do with where you are right now. That's the issue. Your paradigm is what stops you and that's really the purpose of this book: to help you understand what's holding you back from the life you really want.

Setting your type C goal

Once you have your list of wants, choose a goal that's a type C goal. It's something you have no idea how to achieve but you really want. Then write it on a card that you carry with you.

When you decide on your type C goal, you'll probably find it's not in harmony with your paradigms in your subconscious mind. This is where you need to do some work to create that new self-image, a new money paradigm that's in alignment with your goal. Use the decision train (Chapter 5) to discipline your mind until you override that old conditioning.

And as you develop these goals start asking yourself these questions:

- Am I thinking like who I want to be?
- Am I talking like who I want to be?
- If I were a millionaire would I be worrying about this?
- How am I going to grow today?
- Am I acting in harmony with the person I want to be?
- How am I going to give more value today?
- How am I going to improve and give more today?

SUMMARY/TASKS/ACTIONS

- There are three types of Goals
  - o Type A: Something you already know how to do
  - o Type B: Something you think you can do
  - o Type C: Something you really want but have no idea how you'll achieve it
- Teach yourself to focus on what you want
- Start keeping a record of your wins;
- The mind has two parts: Conscious Mind (Knowledge) and Subconscious Mind (Feeling)
- Goals originate in the conscious mind as a thought and you want to impress them over and over on your subconscious mind until you get emotionally involved
- Write a list of your wants
- Create your Type C goal
- Your thoughts cause feelings which inspire you to take action and create the results you want
- Paradigms can stop you from achieving your goals. What new paradigms do you need to create that are in alignment with your goal?

CHAPTER 5 | DECISIONS

"You cannot escape from a prison unless you know you are in one."
Vernon Howard

To create this winning millionaire self-image that you are seeking, you have to learn how to make decisions. It's critical to be able to make a decision, but most people don't actually know how to make one because they haven't been taught either from their parents or at school.

Your decisions were made for you.

Quite often this spans from the clothes that you wore, the food that you ate, the school you went to, what you were taught, the presents you were given and the places you traveled. These were all somebody else's decisions that were made for you.

Subsequently not having known how to make a decision, you're unsure of yourself. You were programmed to literally ask for everyone's advice external to you and then weigh all your options. Sometimes you make the decision and sometimes you don't.

This results in a lack of confidence. I've worked with clients who've had to start with making decisions from a restaurant menu. They were so used to asking the question, "What's everyone else having?" that they never even considered what they wanted. When they first began to make these choices they felt really uncomfortable, because they weren't used to doing it.

Procrastination is the opposite of decision-making. I believe that procrastination is like a disease. It keeps you stuck in the same prison of worry, doubt, fear and lack. Whenever I think of the word procrastination, I think of a picket fence with someone sitting on top of it not going anywhere, getting splinters. Stuck in the same place, not moving forward, not moving back. It's a push pull internal struggle that wastes so much time and energy. The problem is that procrastination has become the way of the world. It's what keeps you exactly where you are. You question things over and over. People who don't know how to make decisions for themselves will continually ask everybody else for their opinion with this question:

What do YOU think I should do?"

This demonstrates a lack of trust in your ability to make decisions for yourself. The better thing would be to ask yourself – What do I think I should do?

Making a decision is so closely linked with your self-image (Chapter 6) that these two chapters go hand in hand. When you have a self-image that doesn't allow you to make a decision, it's linked to your self-worth. Being able to ask yourself what you do want and then make a choice is the first step. If you're in business or a job that requires you to make decisions all the time, it can be exhausting to always be seeking other people's input, weighing all the options when you could make the decision yourself easily and effectively.

Let's look at what a decision is. You can just google this for yourself and you will come up with things like:

- *a conclusion or resolution reached after consideration*
- *the action or process of deciding something or of resolving a question*

The word decision comes from the Latin term:

"To cut from any other possibility"

"When making decisions, you have to learn to make them quickly and change them slowly." This is what the successful people do according to Napoleon Hill. This may go against the grain of everything you've been programmed to believe. The more you understand yourself, the more you understand what you want and the clearer you become about your goal. It becomes easy to make a decision because you'll go within and ask yourself.

This makes the time frame quicker for decision-making because you won't be going outside of yourself for the answer and asking everybody else. Knowing yourself is actually a matter of trust. When you're building your self-image of being a millionaire and focusing on the goals that you want, it's a matter of trusting yourself. Trusting yourself to make the decisions in alignment with what you want.

Continue to ask yourself questions: If I were a millionaire what decision would I be making here? Is this decision taking me further away or closer to my goal? No-one outside of you knows what you really want, which is why it's so critical to know where you're going and keep yourself focused on the target.

What qualities does it require to make a decision? You have to be courageous and you have to be confident. If this isn't part of your self-image, you'll need to build it in. It's actually another decision to move away from the masses and decide to think for yourself. How does a confident person think, feel and act? How would a confident person make a decision?

I love the following quote:

> "Once you have made the decision, you will find all the
> people, resources and ideas you need ... every time".
> – Bob Proctor

And it's true. Bring in some faith here. This is what you need in the recipe of making a decision. Faith in yourself that you've made the right decision for you, and faith that it will take you to where you want to go. Fear and faith both involve you believing in something you cannot see. You probably didn't make decision in the past due to fear. Why not make decisions based on faith? Failing forward is also part of making a decision. You'll make mistakes, give yourself permission to – it's where the real growth lies.

Get clear on what you want and set your goal. Start taking action in alignment with your goal. You only need to take the first few steps. The how will show up and that's where faith comes in. Our logical, analytical, programmed part of the mind has a hard time with this. It wants to know the "whole" how. It's just like driving your car. You know where your destination is and the road is up ahead, but you may only see a few 100 metres in front of you. This is still enough to get you there. Once you grasp this concept, you'll find that making decisions for yourself is part of creating a new habit.

Take a look at your life right now. In the areas of your relationships, your health, your work, your finances, your hobbies, anything. Where are you procrastinating?

What decisions do you need to make for yourself to move forward?

"Successful people make decisions quickly (as soon as the facts are available, and change them very slowly if ever), Unsuccessful people make decisions very slowly and change them often and quickly."

– Napoleon Hill

Let's take this deeper. There are two types of decision – being interested and being committed. I love this quote by Dr Kenneth Blanchard: "There is a different between being interested in creating the life that we want and being committed. When we are interested we do what is convenient, when we are committed we do whatever it takes, we accept only results not excuses."

If you feel like you've made a committed decision to achieve something and you haven't achieved it, there may be a couple of things going on for you.

The decision may have been made in the intellectual part of your mind, but your subconscious part of your mind, where your self-image resides, doesn't believe you can achieve it (This is your paradigm kicking in). As a result, you sabotage yourself or don't actually commit to the decision. You haven't mixed the decision with the feeling and belief that it's truly possible for you to achieve.

This is why working on your self-image and money paradigm is so important.

Having experienced this myself, I know that you must work on the confidence within. And it's not what other people see on the outside. You may hear comments from others that you are confident, amazing and brilliant at what you do. However, if you don't believe this in your core, then you won't achieve what you really want.

Lack of belief and faith will keep you from making the decisions that will propel you forward. It's the internal voice in your head that actually creates the results in your life. If it's not serving you, and you aren't getting the results you want, then some changes need to be made. The first step is to make the decision to change. Then commit to yourself that you'll make the internal changes and do the work on yourself. When you begin, the changes start showing up in your environment and the results will change for you.

The Decision Train

(based on information from Peter Voogds, founder of Gamechangers Academy)

When I first came across this concept of the decision train, I was completely blown away. It's such a simple concept and a great strategy to help you override your paradigms.

Most people aren't achieving to the level that they can and are living a life of regret and frustration. Most people make their decisions based on feeling or their current results, not what's best for them. If they don't feel like working hard, they don't. If they don't feel like working out, they don't. If they don't feel like getting out of bed when the alarm goes off, they don't… and so on. They base their decisions on how they are feeling and then the action is to do nothing. This sets up a cycle of negative feelings, lack of action and poor decisions. It's a self-perpetuating cycle of being stuck.

MOST PEOPLE

| FEELINGS | ⇨ | ACTIONS | ⇨ | DECISIONS |

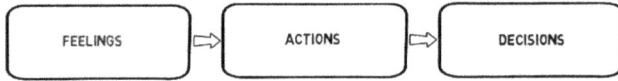

Stressed   Unhappy   Broke   Unhealthy   Regretful
Frustrated   Poor Relationships   Confused

If you want things to change, you have to base things on your decisions. Start basing things from your standards, your visions, and your goals, rather than current circumstances or your feelings. If you don't feel like waking up in the morning, you have to override this (this is your old conditioning, your paradigm).

You made the **decision** to get up early so when the alarm goes off, you take **action** and get out of bed. Then you get to experience the **feeling** of greatness because you followed through. It's the same with going to the gym. I don't always feel like going. But I made the **decision** to work out, whether I feel like it or not. I take **action** and go and then I get to **feel** awesome.

SUCCESSFUL PEOPLE

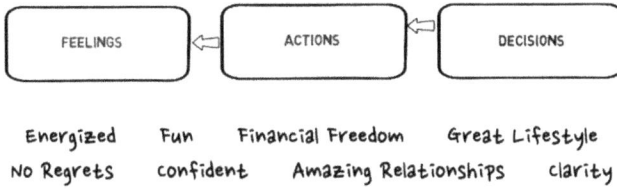

FEELINGS	⬅	ACTIONS	⬅	DECISIONS

Energized   Fun   Financial Freedom   Great Lifestyle
No Regrets   confident   Amazing Relationships   clarity

If you only do what you feel like, you aren't going to do very much. If you want to be successful on your terms, you have to make decisions and take action regardless of how you feel. That's a committed decision and you'll feel amazing afterwards. **Get addicted to the feeling you get after you've completed something**.

Taking action provides results. Different results to what you are experiencing right now. Make a decision to increase your productivity, to take action and override the paradigms that are keeping you stuck where you are. Make your decisions based on who you want to become. Once you have the feeling of accomplishment and reward from taking action, it becomes easier to take the actions as you form a new habit. This creates a new paradigm that's in alignment with the success you desire.

It's the decisions you make daily that determine your reality.

"Never make decisions when you are tired, hungry, frustrated or lonely. I only make decisions when I am in a right state of mind."
– Arianna Huffington of *The Huffington Post*

SUMMARY

- Decisions are linked closely with self-image and confidence
- Make a decision and then take action
- Two types of decisions: interested or committed
- Most people make their decisions based on how they feel
- Successful people make decisions to act first
- Follow the decision train Decision – Action – Feeling
- Make your own decisions and ask yourself – What do I think I should do?

References

1) Peter Voogd's Decision Train, Gamechangers Academy

2) Picture source https://medium.com/@melanylane/whats-your-decision-train-20ee87297087

CHAPTER 6 | SELF-IMAGE

"You never change things by fighting the existing reality. To change something, build a new model that makes the existing model obsolete."
– R. Buckminster Fuller

Self-image is probably the most empowering concept that once understood is your key to everything, to living the life you truly desire. I had been studying personal development fairly intensively for the past seven years or more and never learned about paradigms. The day I learned about paradigms, namely my self-image paradigm, was the day my life changed. Reading this back to myself doesn't convey to you how much this meant to me. I had got to a point in life where I was banging my head against a brick wall and I really didn't think I could do what I was doing for another 40 years. Life changing is an understatement. **You have a control mechanism in your mind and it controls what comes into your life and how well you do, and this is your self-image**.

What is Self-image?

Your self-image is stored in the subconscious part of your mind. It's how you see yourself based upon your genetic and environmental conditioning alongside your own experiences. It's the beliefs and opinions that you hold about yourself. If you're not happy with the results in your life and things aren't changing, this is where you'll need to make some changes and build a new self-image paradigm. You need to understand how your self-image is formed and how it's serving you right now for failure or success.

"Self-image sets the boundaries of individual accomplishment."
– Maxwell Maltz

I love what Maxwell Maltz shares in his book Psychocybernetics – a must read! "Your goals in life are filtered through your self-image, and if they're inconsistent with the self-image, they're rejected or modified. By discovering how to alter your self-image, you end its conflict with your goals."

Getting you from where you are to where you want to be

A person has two self-images. One that the rest of the world sees and the other, which is an internal self-image. The one on the inside is the one that you have to change to improve your results.

The internal self-image acts as the steering mechanism. It's like the GPS of your life, just like the helm of a boat or the bit in a horse's mouth. It leads you through your life whether you realise it or not. If you don't like the results that you presently have in your life. You know your self-image needs an upgrade.

My self-image has completely transformed over the last couple of years since I've become aware of it and what was holding me back. I realised that I had taken on a support role in my husband's life. I was helping him build his dream and vision, but I hadn't stepped into mine because I really didn't know what I wanted to do. I also had to believe I was capable of more.

Ask yourself this question, "Are you the star in your own movie or are you a supporting actor?" I was a supporting actor. This was the first step of acknowledgement for me and then I had to define the movie that I wanted to create for myself. I then began turning my desires into a new paradigm and creating the self-image that was required to do that. This is the work you'll need to do for yourself. Change the opinion you have of yourself. If you're serious about improvements in your life, now is the time to give this your full attention and apply and take action. Create the life script of the movie for the life that you want to be living.

Your External Self-image

Firstly, let's have a look at the self-image you portray to other people. What do they say? Do they tell you that you're confident, focused, handsome, beautiful, disciplined? What other words come to mind? More often than not these are qualities that other people see in you that you don't see or believe about yourself.

I remember distinctly the day when I said to myself, "Maybe I'm the one that's wrong, maybe what everyone else is saying about me is correct." I berated myself for not being good enough. My self-talk was terrible. I realised that maybe I was all those amazing things people said about me. I knew that my way hadn't worked up until now so I decided to start believing what others were telling me (obviously all the good stuff!).

And you know what? It was a complete transformation. Not only did I start thanking people for the complements they were giving me, I also affirmed them in my own mind as well. "Yes, I am confident. Yes, I am a great speaker. Yes, I am attractive." And I could feel the shift in my self-image almost immediately.

Consider your self-mage, what do others say about you in a positive light? What do you believe about yourself? Take a moment and jot these things down. It's really important. (You'll probably find that your paradigm resists you here and tells you to do it later- I guarantee that later will never come – do it now!).

And when you have done, that reflect on what you've written and ask yourself – Is what I think about myself really true?

You have to be really honest and override your old way of thinking. Realise that you aren't as bad as you've made yourself out to be all those years, particularly on an intellectual and physical plane. You have infinite potential, the spiritual side of you is 100% perfect. You've been putting up all these barriers to inhibit you from achieving the success you want and you don't even realise it (the paradigm). These limiting beliefs are completely untrue; they've kept you from having the money you want, the freedom you desire, the health and relationships you want.

Right now, stop believing all those things that just aren't true. It's time to override that inner voice in your head. Reprogram it with thoughts that you want to design a self-image that serves you and delivers the success you desire. Build the new model.

Now that you've identified where you presently are, here are a few things that you can use to start the process toward developing the millionaire self-image you desire.

1. Be kind to yourself

Stop beating yourself up. You need to become your own best friend. That's easier said than done. You must become aware of how you actually talk to yourself and change it. No more berating yourself, calling yourself stupid, dumb or not good enough.

No self-criticism and no complaining. You'd never treat another person the way you treat or speak to yourself, and it has to stop. You have to start treating yourself as the most important person in your life and encourage yourself. If you really cared about someone how would you speak to him or her? How would you care for them? This is exactly what you need to do for yourself. Think about some things you can do to make yourself feel good. How do you like to be treated? What things put you in a good mood? A healthy self-image has you feeling good.

2. Practice receiving

Be open to receiving compliments from others and saying thank you. Accept offers of help rather than pushing them away. It sounds really simple, but if you aren't used to asking for help or accepting offers it can be uncomfortable to begin with.

3. Give value

Be willing to give without expecting anything in return. Give freely and abundantly.

4. Leave everyone with the impression of increase

Make sure you leave every person you come in contact with better off than how you found them. This can be done easily with a smile, a heartfelt compliment, being willing to listen without judgment etc.

5. Have a great attitude

Chapter 2 on attitude goes into great depth here. Get those thoughts, feelings and actions in alignment with the goals you're setting for yourself.

Developing Your Millionaire Self-Image

The mind of a millionaire doesn't think like everyone else. The purpose of this book is to get into the mind of a millionaire and create those thoughts and self-mages in your own mind. Think rich thoughts.

"If you thought the way rich people do, and did what rich people do; do you believe you could become rich too?" is what a friend said to T. Harv Eker.

If you've never been rich before, what thoughts are you meant to be having? What's the new self-image you need to be creating for that millionaire self-image and the financial success that will follow? This is where you need to start challenging the thoughts and beliefs that you currently have. Are they serving you? Are they healthy and helping you go in the direction of your goals or are they actually limiting the success you really want? Millionaires have entirely different thought processes. You began this awareness of thought in Chapter 2 Attitude and you can begin to develop your thoughts even further with your self-image

In building this new millionaire self-image your thought patterns and beliefs need to be evaluated. If they are limiting, then adopt new ones that serve you and will result in the outcome you desire. Create that new model.

Building a new model

- Write out a description of who you want to be with and how you wish to feel
- Work on your self-image and learn to accept and love yourself unconditionally
- Replace any beliefs that don't serve you
- Visualise daily and see yourself in your new self-image achieving your goals
- Take action and be willing to accept opportunities, resources and people that come your way to help you fulfil your goal
- You don't know how long it will take – be persistent and focus on where you're going

Confidence

A millionaire self-image and confidence go hand in hand. Let's explore confidence and find out what it really means and how it's going to help you move forward to your goal. You may be highly intellectual and considered smart, you may have left school early and got a job or began running your business; but if you don't have confidence built into your self-image you aren't going to get where you really want to go. Develop the confidence to make decisions quickly, the confidence to fail forward, the confidence to speak up even when others don't agree with you. And ask for what you want.

Google defines confidence as:

- *the feeling or belief that one can rely on someone or something; firm trust*
- *a feeling of self-assurance arising from one's appreciation of one's own abilities or qualities*
- *a feeling or belief that you can do something well or succeed at something*

Really study those definitions. Read them over and over. How do they relate to you right now? What qualities do you need to build into your self-image to develop self-assurance? You have to align your confidence on the inside with your external confidence. To develop confidence, you have to step outside your comfort zone. You can't keep doing the same thing. You have to take different actions. Really stretch yourself. Understand this is all part of your millionaire self-image. Feel the fear and do it anyway. You'll experience freedom on the other side. When you understand this is a natural part of growth, you'll step forward into it. Otherwise you'll be in the same place one, two or five years down the track. This is where most people stay - in their comfort zones, resisting change. What they aren't aware of is that change is the only constant. We have become a risk adverse world, living in fear of something that 'might happen'.

Understand that when you move toward a goal you'll feel fear and excitement at the same time. That's the indicator for growth. This is where you grow in confidence. That's the sign you need to take that step, whatever it may be.

Can you imagine your life right if you had an internal belief that you could do something well or succeed at something, regardless of what it was? Perhaps getting up and speaking in front of other staff members, putting forward an idea that you think is good. Speaking up and contributing. Acting on that idea in your own business.

If you had this inner confidence about yourself how do you think your life would change? You can do the suggestions in chapter 2 now and align your thoughts, feelings and actions to determine how you need to change your internal image of yourself. You need to act, think and feel with confidence in all areas of your life. Think like a winner, be fearless, assertive, see yourself in a positive light at all times. Be your own cheer squad, believe in yourself.

SUMMARY

- You can't outperform your self-image
- Build a new model and put yourself as the star in your movie
- Build confidence

Further suggested reading

- *Psychocybernetics, The original Science of Self-improvement and Success that has changed the lives of 30 million people.* Dr Maxwell Maltz
- *Art of Acting,* Stella Adler

CHAPTER 7 | FREQUENCY

"Everything is energy and that's all there is to it. Match the frequency
of the reality you want and you cannot help but get that reality.
It can be no other way. This is not philosophy, this is physics."

– Albert Einstein

Now you might be thinking this is a funny name for a chapter in this book. What has frequency got to do with creating more money in your life? Everything.

Frequency, vibration, feelings and energy are all interchangeable in some way. Feeling is another word that has been invented for vibration, and energy is always moving or vibrating. Frequency is what picks up on this energy, vibration or feeling.

I want you to consider this for a moment. Right now, wherever you are there is music playing. Hundreds of compositions: classical, rock, new age, hip hop, etc. It's all there but you can't see, hear it or feel it can you?

However, when you use a radio to tune into frequency, you can choose whichever style of music you want to listen to. Then you can hear it and feel it. Animals can communicate on frequencies as well. Dolphins use echolocation to transmit and pick up communication on a high level of frequency. Just because you can't see it, feel it or hear it doesn't mean it isn't there.

Now consider this. **Your body vibrates at a certain frequency based on the thoughts and feelings you're having**. Stay with me on this. It's really simple and very powerful. I had a complete and utter breakthrough when I understood it. I want you to experience the same.

This frequency can be changed. It all depends on the thoughts you're having. This is incredible. Read this sentence again: **The thoughts you have create the frequency that you operate on. This frequency attracts to you whatever you're in harmony with.**

This will change everything for you when you understand what it means.

Your body is vibrating at a frequency that you can't see but you can feel, right? You know when you're feeling good and you know when you aren't feeling good. Other people pick up on this as well.

I want you to imagine that your body is just like a radio. When you walk into a room you can be either drawn to speak with someone or you can get the feeling you want to avoid someone. You can't quite put your finger on it – it is just a feeling, right?

Become aware of how you feel around other people. Is it the same for everyone? Do you have certain people that you absolutely love being around and always come away feeling alive and energized? Do you spend time with others and come away feeling like it was a real effort and you've had the life sucked out of you, but you aren't sure why?

It's because they're operating on a different frequency, a different radio station. You might be on talk back radio and someone you are talking to is on modern hip-hop and someone else, classical. Depending on your preference, you'll feel a certain way. What you're "listening" to yourself is what you are going to attract to your frequency, your radio station. If you're listening to music that you don't enjoy on a radio station each day are you going to be on the same frequency as the radio station that is playing upbeat, fresh, inspiring songs?

The answer is no.

Think about this.

How you're feeling becomes a frequency that your energy is vibrating on and it becomes a magnet. Like attracts like. If you want different results in your life, like more money and more opportunities, you need to change the frequency you're operating on. You change that frequency by changing the thoughts you're having. Does that make sense?

When developing a millionaire self-image, you have to put yourself on the frequency/radio station of being a millionaire. Now, the really great thing about this is that it's all in your control. You're the one pressing the buttons to the radio station you want to "listen" to. If you don't like it – change it. But how do you change it?

It's really simple which is why so many of us don't actually understand it. You've got to get on to the frequency where you want to be living. The control system behind this is our thoughts.

Control the flow of your thought energy and get yourself onto the right frequency.

Think about the thoughts you're emotionally involved in. Think thoughts of wealth, abundance, freedom and choice. Think thoughts of having that money right now; it showed up in your bank account overnight. It's guaranteed that more is on its way. What would your thoughts be then? How would this make you feel? Even though this isn't true in your physical world you can put yourself on the frequency of having this money just by imagining it.

You have to become really aware of the thoughts you're having and ask yourself: Are they serving me? If not then you have to replace these thoughts with ones that will get you results you want. **Your results then become an expression of your level of awareness.** You have to be really aware of the thoughts that you're having before you can change them. Just look at the results in your life right now. If they aren't what you want, you know you're having some thoughts that are keeping you on a frequency you don't want to be on.

Let me give you an example about success consciousness. While writing this book, I had my own personal breakthrough in shifting my thoughts paradigm. I'd been missing a piece of the puzzle. I'd been experiencing a level of success in my life that I had never experienced before and then it dropped off. I wasn't sure why. The reality was my paradigm had kicked in and I wasn't controlling my thought flow.

This is what happens. Let's watch the paradigm. Let's say you average $3000/week. And then all of a sudden you are making $5000/week or $8000/week. You've stepped out of your paradigm. Your paradigm will to try and pull you back to $3000. You'll start having thoughts like someone who earns $3000/week: "It's a fluke that you were doing that well," "you aren't that good," "It won't last."

That's your inner talk trying to pull you back to $3000. Why is it doing that? – the paradigm doesn't want to die – it wants to stay where it is. You have to be able to ignore your results when they aren't what you want – the self-talk, your thoughts, they'll try to pull you down.

When this happens, just go back to the basics. Go back to focusing on the thoughts and habits you want to create for your success consciousness. Focus on what you want. Create that clear mental image of the goal you desire.

Change the thoughts, change the frequency you're on and change your results.

This is where it begins. You must first think like the person you want to become before you become it. This isn't just about creating your millionaire self-image. This flows over into your health, your relationships, your businesses and the people you spend time with. For example, in a relationship where things aren't going well, the couple has ended up on different frequencies as a result of the thoughts they're having. The paradigm loves this and creates more thoughts that don't serve them and the gap increases.

You've got to get onto the frequency you want to be on and stay there. What's going on in your physical world may be the complete opposite. That's okay, just keep going to that frequency of the good that you desire. Choose thoughts you that allow you to receive the good you desire and just know that it's coming. The chapter on Daily Rituals for Success (Part 3) goes into more detail of what can help you stay on the thought frequency in alignment with your goals.

Because you don't see what's coming, you believe that it's not coming and that changes your frequency you and literally repels the good you desire. Just the way a magnet works. It's either attracting or repelling. Remind yourself to do the illogical, think the illogical.

> *"Fear and faith both require us to*
> *believe in something that we can't see."*
> – Bob Proctor

This is why it's so important to control the flow of the thoughts in alignment with what you desire.

Now, you may build the image of living a millionaire life style, create the self-image and then not focus on it. This is dreaming and won't get you any closer to achieving your goal. When you make this decision to flip your brain and get on to the millionaire frequency, that's when things start to change and the people, resources and opportunities will begin to appear.

What can also happen is that your paradigm can kick in and stop you from thinking on the higher frequency. You end up bouncing from one vibration to another sabotaging what you want. This is why it's so important to be fused with your goal and live from that place. Use your imagination, your will and your focus to stay on the frequency of what you desire. The thoughts and images that you impress upon your subconscious mind control your vibration and your vibration controls what you attract.

The piece of the puzzle that was missing for me was an expectant attitude and getting my thoughts in alignment with this. You'll find yourself continually frustrated and disappointed if your desire isn't combined with expectation.

That's what happens when you don't focus on what you want and focus on what you don't want instead.

You must really believe that your success is guaranteed. When you move toward the goal and the goal moves towards you, it's because you're in harmony with it, you're expecting it. It all comes down to your thoughts. You must really become aware of your thoughts. I had gotten off the track of thinking the right thoughts. My subconscious thoughts were bubbling away from the place of my paradigm. My expectant attitude was focusing on lack and not succeeding again. And that's what was showing up in my results. I started using some prompts to get me back on track – almost becoming a mantra of some sort.

"I am always thinking about what I am thinking about."

"I believe in myself. I believe in my infinite potential."

Then I found the piece of music I'd been searching for that really connected with me. I made a list of success consciousness thoughts that I wanted to have and I began saying them over and over with this music.

I could feel the shift straight away in how I was feeling and my expectant attitude began to change. I needed to create consistency in my thoughts all the time. I also had to look at my results as neutral. Hopefully this is a concept that you can grasp because this helped in shifting my thinking as well. I had been programmed to feel good when my results were good. If I wasn't doing well, I felt bad. My desire was to always succeed and do well. This was fine for the things I could control, but I was living from the outside in. I was completely influenced by the outside circumstances. If I got good results, I felt good.

If you can only feel good when the results are good, you're going to be miserable. I had been doing that to myself and at times I was miserable. I had to change my thinking around this. The results became neutral. Meaning regardless of the result, good or bad I chose to feel good and focus on the thoughts and habits I was creating for the success I was expecting. If you don't get your mind onto that mindset it will eat you up.

Start enjoying the journey. Start looking at it like a game. Start having fun. The game should be how am I improving? How am I getting better? Take each challenge as fun and feel good. When you do this, it gives no energy to your paradigm, it's completely neutralized.

The secret is to get on the frequency of the good that you desire.

"Everything you are seeking is seeking you."

– Rumi

SUMMARY

- Control the flow of your thought energy to get on the right frequency
- Get on the frequency of the good that you desire
- Everything will come to you when you stay on the frequency
- When you change your thoughts, you change the frequency you're on and your results change
- Develop a success consciousness regardless of the results. Results are neutral

CHAPTER 8 | MONEY

"What we really want to do is what we are really meant to do.
When we do what we are meant to do, money comes to us, doors open for
us, we feel useful, and the work we do feels like play to us".

– Julia Cameron

We have an obligation to grow to our greatest potential. And if we can earn more money, this means we can serve and help more people. Imagine if you had learned this from school and your parents. You have an obligation to be rich and do what you love, powerful, right? Well that's what this book is really about. It's helping you unravel the genetic and environmental beliefs that you've been programmed with that are no longer serving you. It's a process of upgrading these thoughts to match the results of being that millionaire that you desire.

Let's take a look at the statement, What is money? Google defines it as:

"a current medium of exchange in the form of coins and banknotes;
coins and banknotes collectively."

Money is an idea. It's a form of exchange. It's a piece of paper or numbers in a bank account. It's not necessarily the million dollars that you want and desire. It's the lifestyle and the freedom that this money provides. Money is just another form of abundance. You can have the same feelings with money that you do for all the other good in your life. It's just this programming we've inherited that has warped our perceptions of how deserving we feel about money.

In Chapter 2 on attitude you were asked to write down your thoughts feelings and actions about money. This helps you get clear about some of your beliefs about money that aren't serving you to create your millionaire self-image. If you haven't done this yet I want you to stop reading right now and do it. There is no point continuing reading this book until you have done that. I used to be one of those people who would skip the exercises and tell myself I would come back and do them, but rarely did. It's critical that you start to become aware of the thoughts you're having around money and determine whether they are serving you or not.

Override the **paradigm** that's telling you to do it later.

- Money is so hard to make/earn
- I never have any money
- I can't afford it
- I repel money
- I don't know how to make money (or when it comes to making money, I'm useless, totally inadequate)
- I'll never make lots of money; I am not smart enough to make lots of money
- I always have bad luck

People without money can justify it to themselves and others by saying, "Money won't make you happy" and "All rich people are greedy."

The key is wealthy people don't think like that. They don't have these thoughts or beliefs.

When I evaluated my attitude about money it shifted my awareness to a whole new level. Our farm had an obvious money pattern of loss over a number of years. This loss was a figure on average that was very similar each year.

We had a mindset that we had to work long hours every day, it was a struggle and there was never enough money. In my own business I found that my income wasn't increasing at the rate I wanted. It basically stayed the same over a three-year period. I didn't really understand it, and I pretty much felt like I was banging my head against a wall. Why couldn't I get ahead? It was a pattern and there was a reason for it. It wasn't just by chance. Understanding paradigms was the missing link. Regardless of what your past results have been with money, you can change them.

I began to really dig deep and analyze my attitude around money.

I became very aware of three things: My money paradigm, my sales paradigm and my self-image. When I looked at my attitude around these three areas it became very obvious why I was stuck.

I wanted to be earning way more than what I was, but found that you can't outperform your self-image. It's directly related to the money you receive. If you don't feel deserving of having money, it doesn't matter how great your thoughts are around it. If I wanted to earn more money, I needed to change my self-image. I began to build a new model and began acting as a person who was earning more money. You'll need to do this too.

"You never change things by fighting the existing reality. To change something build a new model that makes the existing model obsolete."
– R. Buckminster Fuller

There's a part of your mind that needs to be changed for your results to change. It's an inside job of upgrading your thoughts and how you feel about money.

Understanding Money

Do you know that most of the population is trading their time for money and they aren't even aware that there are other ways to make money? The reason they aren't aware of it is because it's not something taught at school or by parents.

There are only three income earning strategies. They are called M1, M2 and M3. Ninety-six percent of the population works with the M1 strategy. This is what we're taught at home and school. It's where you trade your time for money. You get so much an hour or you get a salary for a week or a fortnight. This is a strategy that won't work, but 96 % of the population is following it. If you save any money at all, you're stashing it away, little by little to save for the things you really want. But you're saving this at the expense of your life. This is part of the programming. You never live in the house you want, you don't go on the holidays you want to; you buy the cheapest food on the menu when you go out and you probably never drive the car you want.

This is a losing strategy. There are only so many hours in the day. The problem is it reaches saturation. You can't earn anymore in the job that you're in, regardless of getting a promotion. You're still trading your time for money. If you're following this strategy, don't feel bad about it. Feel excited because you can change it and I am going to share with you how.

The M2 is an excellent strategy and is only used by a small portion of the population where you trade money for money. This is where you invest money into shares or property to get a return on your investment.

The M3 strategy is the one to get excited about. It's what 1% of the population does and they're earning 97% of all the income. Seems absolutely crazy doesn't it? This is the one you need to understand to move you toward that millionaire self-image and bank account.

You may think it's out of balance but it really isn't. It's where you multiply your time by setting up multiple streams of income. If you take a look at successful and wealthy people, you'll find that they all have multiple streams of income.

Working is the worst way to earn money. You have to make the switch in your head to understand that you go to work for satisfaction. That's why it's so important that you love how you spend your days, spend time with people who are successful and enthusiastic; and invest in yourself. This is where you'll have to dig a little deeper. You earn money by providing service. If you're in a job right now, start becoming aware of the ideas that you've been having in the past that you've ignored or pushed to one side. These could be the millionaire ideas that you've had all along, but you weren't aware of them because you've been programmed to have a job and you've settled for that.

This is the income earning strategy that's set up to earn multiple streams of income. Now some of these can be small streams, others larger. You can now do business all around the world and could be earning money while you're sleeping.

This is where your self-image begins to transform when you realise that you can do so much more than what you've been doing. And you have a choice. You can actually do in life what you really want to do. It's just that nobody has given you permission to do that. You've been programmed to go through school and channeled into an area where you could get a good job, possibly based on your grades. You were focused on what you felt you should do, instead of your interests or what you're really good at.

Someone on the outside has steered you in a direction and you probably haven't even asked yourself the question: What do I really want? Personally and professionally? How do I want to be spending my days? How much income would I really like to be earning? If I could wave a magic wand what would my perfect day look like?

]Reaffirm the idea that it's okay to be rich. Disconnect from your belief that you're not like rich people – it's not true. Be rich and be a person of integrity – you can be both.

Moving Forward with a Money Goal

I strongly encourage each and every one of you to have a clear money goal.

For a long time, I had a money goal that I was disconnected from. I didn't have a clear picture of exactly what it looked like; of exactly the feeling it enabled me to harness when I read my goal. I had to really connect with it and when this happens, the picture becomes clearer in your mind and the feeling stronger in your body.

What is it that gets you emotionally involved?

What is the money going to bring you?

What is the difference in your life that it's going to make?

For me, I see myself feeling and allowing, providing all the things that I want for my family: the schools that are the best option for them, travel for my work, my personal development, the home I live in, holidays for my family and being able to give generously and help others. It's also celebrating the success and transformation of my clients.

You have to really fuse with the lifestyle you want to create for yourself. Things won't change unless you're connecting to it, the life that you really want to live. The wording of your goal makes all the difference.

Think of all the things that you can have, rather than can't. You have been conditioned to enter into the spirit of what you don't have. You have to enter into the spirit of what you want to have.

What would you love to be earning and receiving? Every week, every month? Write it down on a piece of paper.

I want you to listen to your inner thoughts right now as you read your goal. I want you to read it out loud and see if there are any counteracting thoughts that are coming up for you.

Be honest with yourself and listen. For example I had this goal and every time I read it I kept having this subconscious feeling that whatever I earned wasn't enough. I felt flat reading my goal because it didn't make me feel financially secure. I didn't feel like my savings was accruing. It didn't matter what was coming in, it was going out. These thoughts that I was having were creating these results in my bank account. Once I realised this, I was able to change it and I did this with an affirmation (I go into more detail in Part 3 Daily rituals for success).

Creating an Abundant Mindset

To change your mindset, you'll have to change your thoughts, your feelings and your actions. Have you ever opened your purse or wallet and thought to yourself, "I haven't got any money." This was certainly a common one for me. It didn't matter if I had money in the bank, it was reaffirming to myself that I didn't have anything in my purse. That was being programmed into my mindset.

Get yourself into an abundant mindset by carrying lumps of cash. I started with $100. It doesn't matter where you start. You can also print out pictures of money and carry that with you. It might sound crazy but it works!

Every time you open your purse or wallet instead of saying in your mind, "I don't have any money," you see this $100 and it reminds you to think abundant thoughts. This really changed my perception and my thought process very quickly. I was able to tell myself "I can afford it." This prosperous mindset started to flood into all avenues where I was spending money and I began to "feel" abundant. It's about creating new thoughts and feelings that are in harmony with having more money.

What do you think your thoughts will be when you open your wallet or purse and see the money? Every time I opened my purse, I said, "I always have plenty of money to do whatever I want."

What you want to do is always feel like you have money. Hold it, carry it, feel it. Because if you're doing that and it feels uncomfortable, then you'll begin to recognise these feelings that are in the way of more money coming to you. You want to be continually changing this relationship with money and being comfortable with seeing it, carrying it and believing you have always have an abundance of money.

If you're a guy, carry money in your pocket with your goal card. I rarely have pockets in my pants or dresses, so I put it in my purse. I have attached my credit cards, goal card and 100 dollar notes with a money clip, so every time I go to pay for something I have the money sitting there. I touch it and feel grateful for the abundance of cash I have.

When I shared this with my clients, I had an interesting response. Someone asked me why I wasn't afraid that someone would steal my money. It was an interesting question because I realised that I probably would have had the same response a few years ago. However, I now know that is the attitude of operating from lack or limitation. You have to flip that thinking to knowing you'll always have money and more is coming your way,

Really concentrate on your thinking around money and how this shows up in your life in other areas. When you're shopping for clothes, groceries or going out for a meal at a restaurant, what are your thoughts? Are they coming from a place of getting what's on special, cheapest or going without? Or are your thoughts telling you that you can afford to have whatever you want? If you don't have the money yet that's okay. It will come as you start to change your thoughts, feelings and actions. It's a matter of creating the feeling of abundance and telling yourself that you have the money now.

Open the Flood Gates to more Money

I used to have on my goal card that my income was coming through my coaching business or through writing my book. Don't limit how the money comes to you. Have an income goal so that you are being open to all the channels that money can come through because you have no idea what's in store. Why suffocate the supply when you can open it up and allow it to come from anywhere?

Who's to say that someone actually gives you a cheque to speak at his or her event next week and they just contacted you last week. Who's to say the government hasn't paid you a return on something – it happened to someone the other day. Allow it to surprise you, allow it to come from anywhere, and be grateful for it.

One of the realizations I had as to why I had limited the money I was receiving, was that I had defined where it was coming in. You may actually have a fear that your business might not work, or you'll never get another job, so you restrict it to come through that channel. Abundance is a completely different mindset. There is no lack, no fear with abundance. It's about allowing it to come in from anywhere. Never suffocate the supply.

In the past when I didn't carry cash, I could never give it away to a donation or charity when I felt the urge to give something. I always had the excuse that I didn't have cash on me. What had I been affirming over and over and over in my mind? That I didn't have any money! It really made me realise how that was coming from a lack mindset. When you flip onto that abundant thought frequency, more money will come your way.

I didn't realise that at the beginning and I didn't have a specific money goal. These are all things that will come for you as your awareness continues to grow. Money can come through Multiple Streams of Income (MSI), through a gift, through an offer to buy you dinner/lunch, through your business, work etc.

It's important to recognize and be grateful for whichever form money comes in. You might be looking for it in cash, but the more grateful that we are for it in any form, we can open our awareness to seeing it and receiving more.

It really is that simple. Change your thoughts to be in harmony with the money you desire. This is critical to increasing your income in your business, your work and allowing money to come from all different sources. Be open to receiving money as well. Allow people to pay for you. Offer to pay. Don't be that person that stands back hoping that someone else will cover you. Lots of simple little things add up to either a lack or the millions you're seeking.

The Money is already here

Your income and what you want to be earning is right here. I may really challenge your thinking in this section, but be open to it. The trick is not to be fooled by what you can't see. Don't live through your senses and think that's it. One of the biggest issues and problems I've seen with a lot of people, including myself is thinking it's almost here. No, it's not almost here. It's not outside of you – it's actually here now. You've already got it. That might take a little bit to play with in your mind, because your subconscious programming is telling you the complete opposite.

But to think you already have it … Where is it – I can't see it in my bank account? That exact thinking is keeping you where you are. If you keep looking at your bank account seeing debt and not enough – those are the thoughts you're having, what you're focusing on and you're going to get more of that.

So, stop thinking like it's outside of you. Because as long as you keep thinking like that it will always stay outside of you. And you're always going to feel like you're almost there.

Why not upgrade your thoughts, use your imagination and feel like you already have it? Why don't you feel like it's in your account now? That you've received the income you want, that you're living in the house you want, you're going on vacations that you really want and you're fusing with that feeling.

It really is all about frequency (Chapter 7). What you've currently been operating from with your income is on this frequency. The income on your goal card is on an abundant frequency. The only way you're going to attract that income into your life is by thinking and feeling from that frequency.

You can't let what your five senses are telling you dictate how you feel. It's not the easiest thing to do by any stretch. We've been conditioned to live from the outside in. What we need to do is fuse with the feeling that we already have it now and live from the inside out.

You've just been paid. Your income is where you want it to be Your savings is where you want it to be. You're living the life you've always wanted. And that's a different feeling. Operate with your thoughts and feelings on the abundant frequency. Know that you'll keep dipping when you're starting to change and upgrade your mindset– that's okay, it's the paradigm that's in the way. You're overriding your old conditioning. Because you can't see it in front of you doesn't mean anything. Absence of evidence is not evidence of absence.

You need to know what people are doing to create wealth and follow their example: What do they read? What drives them? What do they wear? How do they present themselves? How do they stay motivated and excited? Build this into your millionaire self-image.

Fall in love with helping people and the money will follow. Choose to enjoy your life right now. Be grateful for all the people, resources and opportunities in your life – that's the key to bringing more into your life. Money is just one part of wealth. But when you have money, you'll realise how much more time you have because you aren't worrying about money.

"Wealth is the ability to fully experience life."
Henry David Thoreau

SUMMARY

- Review your attitude about money (Chapter 2)
- Provide more service doing what you love
- Have a money goal and connect with the feeling of already having that money
- You can't outperform your self-image
- There are three income strategies
  - o M1 Trading time for money (96% population)
  - o M2 Using money to make money (3% of the population)
  - o M3 Multiple streams of income or MSI (1% of the population does this, you can do it too!)

Recommended Reading

- *Attract More Money Now* – Joe Vitale
- *It's Not About the Money* – Bob Proctor
- *Money is God in Action* – Raymond C Barker
- *The Prophet of Profit* – Jacquelyn MacKenzie

Money Affirmations

- I respect money and money loves me
- I have a wonderful relationship with money
- As I circulate money, it comes back to me multiplied
- My income and savings are constantly increasing
- I love that my profits are constantly and dramatically increasing
- I am so happy and grateful now that money comes to me in increasing quantities, from multiple sources on a continuous basis
- I am wise with my money
- I am a money magnet
- I have an abundance mindset
- It feels so good to be financially wealthy

- It's so easy for me to attract so much money
- I have amazing money paradigms
- I am so happy and grateful now that I am attracting opportunities and people who want to work with me and I am aware when they are present
- Every day in every way my wealth is increasing
- I always have more money coming in than going out
- I love money and money loves me
- There is an abundance of money and it's on its way to me
- I am attracting more and more money every day
- I am receiving more money today

CHAPTER 9 | DISCIPLINE

"The discipline of writing something down is the first step toward making it happen."

Lee Iacoca

Discipline creates your lifestyle and consistent discipline separates the extraordinary from the average. Self-discipline is doing the right thing whether you feel like it or not. This is the single most important skill to learn if you want to create the success you desire.

I knew I had a problem when I was unable to review my weekly goals and read my goal every day. I had started a course, which didn't allow me to go on to the next module unless I completed set tasks. I couldn't complete these tasks daily or weekly tasks and thought to myself – *What's wrong with me?* I did go on to the next modules, but felt that I was cheating myself. I couldn't master a simple task and I didn't know why. I considered myself a disciplined person and on appearance I was. Introducing this new habit into my life was going in the right direction, but I just couldn't make myself do it.

When I learned about paradigms my whole world changed. I was able to adhere to doing these daily rituals. My subconscious programming had been limiting my ability to create these habits and I was continually sabotaging myself. With the understanding of paradigms, I knew why I couldn't complete daily and weekly rituals in the past.

My awareness that there wasn't anything wrong with me and that I could change was a real eye opener. I realised my paradigm was pulling me back – that's why I hadn't been able to persist with these daily and weekly habits even though I knew they were part of the success routine of wealthy people. I needed to build them in to my self-image and I could feel the resistance.

I realise now that there were a couple of things going on for me. The desire wasn't there, the belief in myself was missing and I was self-sabotaging. I had a burning desire for success, but I wasn't emotionally connected with my goal. This connection came about when I was able to identify what I really wanted and then imagine myself having it. **I had to connect with the feeling of myself having it and this took time and daily discipline, which I didn't have and had to create.**

Connection with the feeling of achieving my goals didn't come easily to me. I had to really build this muscle to create a clear mental picture and then connect it with the thoughts and feelings of having it now.

As you delve into Part Three of this book, you'll realise this is the most important thing that you'll be doing: Connecting with the feeling of already having achieved your goals, dreams and desires, and creating an expectant attitude of receiving it. The daily rituals help you do this.

I knew that I had to overcome my resistance to pursue what I wanted in my life and what I really knew I was capable of achieving. I had to make the committed **decision** to be persistent and create productive actions around my goals. I had to invest in myself and get a mentor who had already got to where I wanted to go. I knew that it was possible for me and it is for you too.

This quote from Bob Proctor, "*Discipline is the ability to give yourself a command and then follow it*," became my mantra. I knew that I had to make these rituals and habits part of my daily life and be disciplined about them. And I kept seeing these quotes

> "*Your level of success is determined by your level of discipline and perseverance.*"
>
> – Anonymous
>
> "*Without self-discipline, success is impossible, period.*"
>
> – Lou Holtz
>
> "*Discipline is the bridge between goals and accomplishment.*"
>
> – Jim Rohn

*"You'll never change your life until you do something daily.
The secret of your success is found in your daily routine."*

– John C Maxwell

*"The ability to discipline yourself, to delay gratification in the
short term in order to enjoy great rewards in the long term, is the
indispensable prerequisite for success."*

– Maxwell Maltz

The synchronicity of seeing these quotes was a great confirmation that I was on the right track. I knew that I had to break through my conditioning and make specific daily rituals a habit every day. I knew they were part of my pathway to success.

It starts with the little things

"How you do one thing is how you do everything." I absolutely loved this YouTube video and wanted to share it with you. It really demonstrates how important daily disciplines are and the feeling of success that follows. It's a Navy Seal Admiral talking about lessons for success He talks about making your bed and the discipline that's instilled in military people. It can be perceived as a little thing, but it's really a big thing.

Every morning if you want to change the world, start off by making your bed. Every morning in Seal training, my instructors, who were all Vietnam veterans, would show up in my barracks room and the first thing they did was inspect my bed. If you did it right the corners would be square, the covers would be pulled tight, the pillow centered just under the head board and the extra blankets folded neatly at the foot of the rack.

It was a simple task, mundane at best. But every morning we were required to make our bed to perfection. It seemed a little ridiculous at the time, particularly in light of the fact that we were aspiring to be real warriors, tough, battle-hardened seals, but the wisdom of this simple act has been proven to me many times over. If you make your bed every morning, you will have accomplished the first task of the day. It will give you a small sense of pride and it will encourage you to do another task and another and another. And by the end of the day that task completed will have turned into many tasks completed. Making your bed will also reinforce the fact that the little things in life matter. If you can't do the little things right, you'll never be able to do the big things right. And if by chance you have a miserable day, you'll come home to a bed that is made. That YOU made. And a made bed gives you encouragement that tomorrow will be better. So, if you want to change the world, start off by making your bed.

https://youtu.be/KgzLzbd-zT4
University of Texas at Austin 2014 Commencement Address –
Admiral William H. McRavenTexas Exes

Aren't these wise words? Do you make your bed each day? I do, as soon as I get out of it. Not because I want to – but because it has become a habit. It's certainly not up to military standard, but what this man says is true – it does provide a sense of achievement. Now if this isn't a habit of yours, make it a goal to implement it and then you can turn to the list of rituals I'm going to share with you.

Understand that there's a reason why 1% of the people have 97% of the money in the world and why not everyone is a millionaire. There are certain habits that successful people do and the following story by Peggy McColl is a perfect example of this. (Peggy McColl is a world-renowned expert, a *New York Times* Best-selling Author, an internationally recognized Speaker/Author/Mentor and an expert in the area of goal achievement).

Peggy attended a conference in Hawaii in the mid 90s – it went for very long hours sometimes going from 8am till 11pm or later. "I remember the speaker who was on stage, and he said, "for those of you that are hungry and committed, I am going to do a special bonus session for you tomorrow morning out by the pool."

We were at the Hilton and when he made that bonus session for 7am I remember thinking, "Oh my goodness, we're hardly getting any sleep." By the time we're finished for the day everyone is exhausted. I was thinking this is a big offer to the people in the room. There were about 1100 people. I wondered, "where are all these people going to sit? How are they going to get them around the pool? It's a good size pool, but 1100 people?

I decided I was one of those hungry, committed individuals and I would be there for the 7am special bonus session, even though we were only getting a few hours sleep. I went back to my room, set my alarm, got up a little early and headed to the pool I wanted to get up early because I thought I probably won't even find a spot to sit. I got to the pool early and there was no-one there.

I thought, "Did I get it wrong, have I got the right pool, the right date, did I get the instructions wrong?"

Within a matter of a few minutes, the instructor arrived at 7 sharp. There were maybe 20 people around the pool. I remember thinking, "Oh my goodness, where are all the rest of the people?" I guess they were sleeping. It reminded me of just how the opportunities in life are available to everyone. What I found being at this meeting is so few people really follow through.

How many people simply just don't follow through?

I had to get the calculator out right away when I heard this story. Those 20 people made up only 1.66% of the people. All 1100 were all offered the same opportunity. Are you prepared to do what it takes to reach your success? You have to do what this 1.66 % of people did. Make it a habit to say yes to the opportunities that come your way.

This is why it's never crowded along the extra mile: Most people aren't willing to do the things that successful people do.

SUMMARY

- Discipline has to be built into your self-image if you want to succeed
- Doing little things every day creates success habits
- Discipline is the ability to give yourself a command and follow it
- You have to create the habit of discipline and do things that you don't feel like doing
- Daily discipline is key to overriding the paradigms that aren't serving you

PART TWO

CHAPTER 1 | BRIAN MATSEN

Currently: Mindset and Business Coach at Brian Matsen Coaching

Brian lives in California. He was a Regional Vice President with ING and an investor when he made his first million dollars at the age of 32.

Brian's story had me sitting on the edge of my seat as he shared some of the key events through his childhood and early adulthood that shaped his millionaire mindset. He's also one of the most humble people I've met and has a real willingness to help others.

Some common themes throughout his story are: it's necessary to know exactly what you want, make a decision, be laser focused and always serve others. Understand that there will be obstacles that you'll face, but they'll help you get where you want to go.

Brian's Story: Growing Up

My parents were very positive, hardworking people. Their examples have been instrumental to my success from day one. My dad is an attorney and my mom was a schoolteacher (she passed away shortly after I was married). They were always striving to be the best they could be. I owe much of my positive mindset to them.

My Dad would say to me, "Brian, you've got to pay the price." This meant if you want to be good or successful at anything you need to put forth effort and do the work. You must be willing to do the things you don't always want to do, even when they aren't comfortable or easy. You also must do things other people aren't willing to do. It's the common denominator of success.

My parents taught me from a young age that I could accomplish anything because of who I am. I am a child of God made in his image. My spiritual DNA is perfect, therefore I have unlimited potential to be and do anything. There's nothing more powerful or meaningful than having this knowledge. It has brought me strength and comfort throughout my life.

Deciding not to go to school in first grade

When I started first grade, I didn't care too much for my teacher. I decided I wasn't going to attend class anymore. When my mom would leave for work in the morning and drive down the street, I'd walk in the opposite direction and wait around the corner until she was gone. I'd come back to the house and do whatever I wanted all day. For a whole week, I ate ice cream, watched TV, and had a great time. My next-door neighbor Mrs. Ballog noticed I was staying home and told my mom. My mom couldn't believe it. Mrs. Ballog offered to help her out by driving me to school. When we arrived, she said I had two options, I could either go straight to class or I could meet with the principal.

I decided to talk to the principal. Mrs. Ballog was shocked I had chosen to meet with him. She only gave me that option because she was sure I'd be too scared to talk to him. She was wrong! I went in and explained to the principal why I didn't want to go to school. (Remember, I was only 6). He said, "Brian, you don't have a choice. If you don't go to school, you are breaking the law and you can get into big trouble."

He managed to scare me with the whole breaking the law thing, so I finally went to class. But no one could believe I took the meeting with the principal rather than going to class or that I'd chosen to skip school in the first place. My mom was so embarrassed because the principal was her former boss, yet she was very impressed her son possessed such confidence at a young age. The principal's words had such a big effect on me that it lasted all the way until third grade when I did it again.

Authors note: I think the key to this story is that Brian made a decision about what he wanted and acted upon it. This tenacity has served him well in his career and business.

Getting my Driver's Permit

When I turned fifteen years old, I remember how excited I was to get my drivers permit. Unfortunately, my parents wouldn't let me get it because my grades weren't good enough. I wanted my drivers permit so bad and nothing was going to stop me from getting it. So, I made a **decision**. I rode my bike to another city, twenty miles each way, so I could attend driving school. For weeks, my parents had no idea what I was doing.

After completing the course, I took the test and passed. I asked my instructor to sign on my parent's behalf, so I could get my permit. I remember bringing it home to my parents and explaining what I had done. Instead of getting mad at me, they were impressed and blown away that I would go to those lengths to get my permit. They couldn't believe the tenacity and persistence I demonstrated. It's just something inside of me… when I truly want something; I do whatever it takes to make it happen.

Becoming the best high school shooter in basketball

I've always had a great love and passion for sports. When I was a kid, I made a **decision** to become the best high school shooter in Orange County, CA. It had a population of about two and a half million people with hundreds of thousands of kids. I held that image in my mind. I practiced and played hours and hours of basketball. I was either in a gym or in my front yard shooting baskets every single day.

In my senior year of high school, I shot 58% from the floor, the best field goal percentage for any guard. I was also the number one free throw shooter in Orange County. Twenty-seven years later, I still hold the free throw record at my high school. I remember placing that image into my mind years before and it taught me a great lesson – when you have a goal and put your mind to something, it will become reality. I recognized this was how my mind worked. This experience helped me develop a success mindset and winning attitude.

Missionary Work

Soon after high school, I served a two-year volunteer mission for The Church of Jesus Christ of Latter-day Saints in Puerto Rico. I knew very little Spanish when I arrived.

I was assigned a companion to work with throughout my mission. On my first day in Puerto Rico, we went to a family's home to teach them. I remember my companion turned to me and said, "You're going to teach the lesson." I was thrown into the deep end right from the beginning. I was scared to death but had to face my fears head on. Every day I had to approach strangers and strike up conversations… and I had to do it in a foreign language. I remember feeling so uncomfortable, but it got easier as each day passed.

My mission experience became the foundation of my adult life and future success. I learned about self-discipline, overcoming rejection, study habits, goal setting, the importance of hard work and serving others. I wouldn't trade those two years for anything. It was far more valuable than any formal education I ever received.

Authors note: I remember Brian sharing this story at an event and it gave me so much understanding as to how and why he loved sales, and why he was so good at it. He faced fears of rejection, of speaking to people daily, learning another language, and of people saying no to him from a very young age. This built Brian's resilient mindset with a purpose of serving others.

From Career struggle to Success

I graduated from Utah Valley University with a Bachelor's degree in Business Management. The first five years after graduation, I really struggled. My career didn't unfold like I thought it would and I faced some real obstacles.

My first job was with a sports related dotcom company in Utah. I thought I was in heaven, until I learned the company was engaging in unethical business practices. I made a decision to quit working for the company.

I moved home to California and started selling life insurance. Within a year, I realised it wasn't the path I wanted to follow. I started to doubt myself and my confidence was at an all-time low. I was in a real slump and I had to pull myself out of it. I stopped feeling sorry for myself and went out and found a job with a marketing company in Utah. This job led me to a better opportunity in Arizona six months later. I was feeling good about things again and I was gaining back my confidence. After two years, I was asked to leave, and a short time later, the company went out of business.

I realised at this stage of my life I was just drifting. I wasn't passionate about any of my jobs up to that point. I was however, extremely grateful at that time for my success as a missionary and as an athlete. I knew because of these experiences, I could overcome the challenges I was facing. I knew I needed to have the same focus in my career as I did with my missionary work and basketball.

I was ready to make a major change. I decided I had to find something in an industry that I enjoyed. That was the day I made a decision to go back into the financial industry, but this time I would focus on investments and not insurance. I had learned about investing and the stock market while in college. I really wanted to pursue a career in investments, which made a world of difference.

Over the next year, I worked as a financial advisor. During this time, I discovered a specific career within the industry which encompassed both my love for investing and for public speaking. It was a perfect match. I saw the large amount of money people in this career were making and realised I was just as talented as they were. I asked myself, "Why not me? Why can't I have this?" I made a decision to make it happen. I became laser focused. Like the decision I made when I got my drivers permit, nothing was going to stop me.

A short time later, I was introduced to ING and took a position with their asset management unit. It wasn't the job I ultimately wanted, but it was a necessary stepping stone. I didn't always enjoy what I was doing, but I knew it was the price I had to pay to get to where I wanted to go. Exactly one year later I was made a Regional Vice President over the Midwest in Chicago.

I remember driving down the freeway in Scottsdale, Arizona when I received the call from my boss informing me I had the job. I was beyond excited! I was yelling, "Yes!" at the top of my lungs. I knew at that moment my life was never going to be the same. It was an incredible feeling. My future was bright, and I never looked back.

Once I made the decision to make it happen, it took one year to reach my goal. It takes most people five to seven years if it all, to become a Regional Vice President. I started making six, eight and ten times the amount of money I was making before. My money paradigm continued to change. My belief in myself was rock solid. **Within a short period of time, I had turned my annual income into my monthly income.**

One thing I attribute more than anything else to getting this job was my time as a missionary. I remember most of my interview with the CEO was spent talking about my mission experience. I woke up at 6:30 am and studied for two hours every morning. I worked extremely hard all day and served late into the night. He later told me this was the main reason he offered me the position. He was extremely impressed with my commitment and knew it would translate to my performance as a Regional Vice President.

*Authors Note: **Why not me?** These three words are very powerful. I've applied them to my life and my clients' lives since hearing Brian's story. I encourage you to do the same. Start applying them to your own life and what you want to achieve.*

Personal Development and Money

I didn't always have a positive money paradigm. I was confident in many areas, but not when it came to money. I grew up with divorced parents. I lived with my mom and two siblings. My mom was a school teacher therefore, money was always tight in our household.

My money paradigm began to change when I purchased my first home. This was about two years before I started working for ING. At that time, I also began studying personal development. Although I didn't apply everything I learned, my mind was beginning to open to new possibilities. As I changed my thoughts, my results improved.

Two years later, I sold my first home for a significant gain. I immediately bought another home and again sold it for a nice profit. My financial status was shifting. I was beginning to understand I could make money outside of my employment. These real estate transactions would provide me with capital for future investments.

Once I was made Regional Vice President in Chicago, my focus intensified. I became a voracious reader. I read and studied every day (and still do to this day.) I wanted to know what it would take to become a millionaire. Except for my house, I was debt-free. I decided I wanted to be completely debt-free, so I set a goal to pay off my mortgage. I read that if I was very disciplined, I could pay it off in seven years. As often happens when you go after something you really want, I was able to achieve it much faster. It only took me four years. I was a debt-free millionaire.

Not only was I making more money from my career, I also was making money from other sources of income (creating MSIs that I mentioned in Part 1 Chapter 8). I invested in real estate, the stock market and other entrepreneurial ventures. I even purchased a beach front condo in Costa Rica for my family to enjoy. My world expanded as my money paradigm changed.

My perception of money changed when I realised many people I respected and admired were wealthy. These individuals were able to give so much to others around them. They were also able to have influence and provide service far beyond their physical presence. **I learned from them that money is a magnifier. If you're already a good person and you achieve financial success, you'll become a better person.**

No matter how much money I make, I always obey the law of tithing. This law requires us to give ten percent of our income or increase. Like all universal laws, when you obey it, you receive blessings. As I made more money, I was able to give beyond ten percent. A few years prior, I had been living paycheck to paycheck. Now here I was able to help others in financial need. I realised how awesome it was to have enough money to provide not only for my family, but also to assist other people. For example, I helped a young man pay for his two-year mission for our church. I knew how important my missionary experience was and wanted him to have the same opportunity.

When I was growing up, my mom and I use to drive around a beautiful neighborhood with big custom homes and dream of owning one. When I was in high school, I had several friends who lived there. I loved spending time in their homes. I thought to myself, "One day I am going to live here." Three years ago, I moved back to California and decided to buy a home in that neighborhood. Now I live where I dreamed of living as a kid and I'm raising my own children here.

I used to think if I were to make a lot of money it would mean I was not focusing on the right things. That isn't true. It wasn't a healthy paradigm. I don't love money. I never have. I love people. Money is a commodity. A very important one, I might add. If anyone tells you differently don't listen to them. Just about everything we do revolves around it. Earning a substantial amount of money has not only allowed me to provide for my family and help others, it has given me freedom. Freedom to spend time with my family and friends. Freedom to travel to places I've always wanted to visit. Freedom to do things I've always wanted to do. The list goes on. If I didn't have the money, I would have missed out on many of my most treasured memories.

The personal growth that has taken place on my journey is priceless. It's all about the person I've become. I remember the day I became a millionaire. I thought it was going to be an amazing day, but it wasn't much different from the day before. No bells, whistles or celebrations. I remember calling my Dad to tell him, but that was it. Some people think when they become a millionaire they're suddenly going to be super happy. That's not the case. **Happiness can be had all along the way if you're doing something you love.**

Brian's Recipe for Success

You must have an ambitious **goal** and stay laser **focused**. Never let anything stop you from achieving it. Life is full of obstacles and challenges, but you must be persistent. Have **faith** and **confidence** in yourself. Other people can believe in you but at the end of the day, you must believe in yourself. You will not achieve your goal unless you **believe** and **expect** it to happen.

Choose a goal you are excited and passionate about. It must be something you've never achieved before. You may have thought about this goal in the past, but never gave it serious consideration. Make a committed decision to accomplish it and dive in immediately. The path toward your goal won't always be easy or enjoyable. There will be times when you don't feel like working at it, but it's necessary to take action anyway.

Procrastination is a killer. It wastes time and energy. Too many people live in a world of fear and indecision. Don't fall into this trap. When you continuously push off necessary tasks, it creates chaos in your mind and decreases your self-confidence.

Most people don't have enough **confidence** in themselves. They don't believe they can do what they're capable of doing. It's essential to implement positive habits into your daily routine. Start with small changes. This will help you build momentum and **confidence**. The sky's the limit, it's just a matter of what we want to **believe** about ourselves.

We all have an imagination making it possible to reach into the future and bring our dreams into the present. Every day visualise your goal already being achieved. Let both your mind and body internalize and emotionalize your desired result. The goal becomes real because you have lived it inside your mind.

Additional daily habits to help you win:

• Study Daily

• Pray

- Exercise
- Eat healthy
- Get enough sleep
- Get up early
- Give Gratitude
- Be of Service
- Get a mentor

What's Next?

I made a decision in 2017 to leave my prosperous financial career to become a mentor and coach to individuals and companies. Helping them achieve results they never thought possible is my greatest reward.

SUMMARY

- Know what you want, something you really desire
- Visualise your goal in your mind and take action
- Discipline
- Mindset
- Serving other people
- Faith
- Decisions
- Laser Focus
- Obstacles, problems are part of the process of developing
- Get outside your comfort zone

CHAPTER 2 | SUSAN HUM-RATCLIFF

Susan lives in Canada and made her first million when she was 36.

The greatest insight Susan gained over her life was that she's no different from anyone else in this world. She doesn't have super powers or have any advantages that enabled her to achieve great success. What she has achieved she believes anyone can do. It's just a matter of priorities and choice. Her focus was growth through personal development. She spent her life studying her own actions and results, acknowledging her fears and then taking every action to overcome them by facing them head-on. Change became her best friend and she became very comfortable in the uncomfortable.

What is interesting about Susan's story is she created much of her success based on her intuition.

Life-Shaping Events

I was a medical laboratory technologist and was working in a micro-biology laboratory in Canada when I was 22. I left for Hong Kong with a friend when I was 24 with only $1000 in each of our pockets. I didn't even consider that $1000 does NOT go very far in Hong Kong and ran out of money within three weeks of our arrival.

I then found out that I couldn't work in Hong Kong because I needed a University qualification and licenses that I hadn't completed in Canada. I had no working visa, I was 24 years old and I couldn't work in the medical industry.

After running out of money, my friend and I only had two choices, to return home or stay. We decided to stay. This was truly the beginning of my journey. It was an easy choice for my girlfriend as she was born in Hong Kong and can get a job anytime which she did. She got a job in a brokerage firm within a week. I, however, had to think fast and think creatively. It wasn't as simple for me as I didn't have the ability to work in Hong Kong because I wasn't born there. To make things even more challenging, I didn't complete my University degree and I didn't speak Cantonese. I remember thinking to myself, "I will make it happen, I will stay… I'm not going back to Canada!"

The first day my girlfriend left for work, I was alone in that old, awful apartment for the first time in weeks. I had no choice but to get moving and start thinking fast. I immediately went down to the newspaper stand, got myself the only English newspaper, *The South China Morning Post*, bought myself a cheap Chinese breakfast bun and went straight into the job search. That was the first official day of my 11 years in Asia.

My first and only interview was with a well-known Australian fitness, health and beauty company called Phillip Wain. The easiest way for me to get a job was to use my personality. All I needed was to get my foot in the door. I got hired right after that first interview for the role of administrative assistant. I jumped on it, even though it was low pay in Hong Kong terms. Phillip Wain owned fitness spas throughout Asia that mainly catered to movie stars and upper class people. It was incredible that I even got a job there. I was double the size of those Chinese girls. They were all so tiny they made me look obese. I was hired to be the go-between from the local staff to the management team who were all westerners. One slight problem, I didn't speak Cantonese. Thank God I had strong enough self-esteem to withstand the judgements.

I retired at the age of 46. It took me 20 years to reach my goal of retiring as a millionaire before I turned 50. The difference for me was that money isn't my biggest driver – it's actually empowerment. I knew that when I verbally expressed my dream of having it all before 50 that I had no idea how I was going to achieve this.

Financial Planning and its Impact on me

The circumstances I was born into revolved around struggle and limitations. My parents had no freedom, they were bound to 14 hour work days, 365 days a year in our family restaurant. I was taught limitations from a very young age. I was bullied on a societal level through racism and prejudice. Poverty is what we knew and survival was what I should have striven for. None of this stopped me from pushing those boundaries, those externally imposed limits. I didn't have a clue how I was going to get to my dream, but I knew it was going to happen and I was willing to do everything to get there.

I was 25, living in Hong Kong and I met with a financial planner. I didn't know anything about money or finances except I overspent for the wrong reasons. I was spending more money than what I was earning.

He asked me two questions that changed my life forever.

1) *When do you want to retire?*

   I told him, "I don't know at 25 how are you supposed to know." I told him 25, laughed and then said 50 years old. I really didn't know what he was doing. But I decided on the age of 50 or before.

2) *How much do you want to have when you retire?*

   I said "I don't know you're supposed to tell me that." Then I said, "A million dollars." I don't come from a million dollar background and this was a life-changing moment. My parents own a Chinese restaurant and if I didn't go down the path I did going to Hong Kong, I would've owned a Chinese restaurant. I'd be serving you Chinese right now! And I'd be the bitterest Chinese person serving you chicken chow mein and yelling at you, because I'd hate what I'm doing! When I said a million in my mind I thought, "How the hell is that ever going to happen because I can't save… I love to spend!"

He worked backwards from there, of course. He responded, "OK Susan, this is how much you are going to have to deposit into the investment account so we can help you grow"

I thought to myself, "This amount is much more than I'm making now. This isn't really going to work."

I remember at that life-defining moment it just changed something in me. I never focused on it, but I became very ambitious. I really focused on getting a job number one. Working on myself, number two. Working on my self-confidence, my self- worth, everything that had to do with me.

Self-Image

I was very single at that time. I had to be because I had a 10 year rela-tionship from the age of 13 to 23 which wasn't a good idea. I had a lot of self-development work to do on myself so I focused on my career, my relationships, and friends. I focused on everything.

I observed that most people in their twenties want dependency. They want to be with somebody, to have a boyfriend/girlfriend and get married. So many women around me were desperate and single and we couldn't even have dinner together and talk about things without them checking out potential husbands.

I couldn't stand that so I chose to focus on myself. The relationships will come when you know what you want. I knew I had to work on myself and my self-worth. That was a big catalyst that got me from where I was to where I am today.

None of this was a conscious thing for me. I just took a really good look at myself in the mirror and I didn't really like what I saw looking back. I was highly manipulative. I cheated on every boyfriend I'd ever had, it was just terrible. I realised I needed to change subconsciously. I knew it was a pattern I didn't want to continue. It was one of those things that if somebody had made me understand, I probably would have made it happen faster.

I became **aware** that I needed to change.

It's illogical, but I focused on the negative things about myself and determined what I needed to change. Society teaches us to avoid anything negative. That didn't feel right to me. Instead of avoidance, I faced negative thoughts and negative events with a different mindset. I transmuted the negative into constructive and positive thoughts. I focused on the negative because I really got to know the person I didn't want to be. So, what I did was quite different.

This is where I go against a lot of the philosophies where the awareness is taking into account all the negatives. It's not about ignoring the negatives. My motivating factor was that I didn't want to be where I was. For me to focus on the person I wanted to become, I wanted to really understand who and where I was. Most people don't talk about that. **We have to be friends with what we don't like about ourselves first and then we determine where we want to be after.**

Authors note: Susan really became aware of who she was and who she needed to become to earn that million dollars for retirement. She figured out what was working and what wasn't. Susan made a decision to change because she was dissatisfied with her results.

That was the catalyst and everything else just fell into place because I made a decision: I am not going to be that person. Then I created what I wanted.

One of the cardinal rules of authenticity is that you have to walk your talk. People watch behaviours, people don't hear words. Integrity is everything and most people don't understand what that word means. **Integrity speaks the truth always and you have to understand what that truth is first of all.** You have to see what your behaviour is verses what you say. That's when you know your truth. Is it aligned with your actions or not?

It could have gone either way with my self-image. I hit as high as 192 lbs (85kgs when I was working in the fitness industry which was pretty ironic).

I became friends with the senior sales director. She was doing all the campaigns for the company and decided I was a prime candidate for their one-year campaign to lose weight. I had to do before and after photos and be on a strict regime of food and exercise. But they couldn't control me and I couldn't control me. They could control my eating and all my exercise and all the slimming treatments, but as soon as I got unleashed at 6 o'clock, it was party time and the regime went out the window.

I ended up gaining extra weight over that eight months before they weighed me in so they had to switch the program before and after photos!

My **paradigm** just kicked in – don't tell me what to do. And I just let go.

Paradigms can work for and against you. With my weight it was definitely against me. But with my career my paradigm propelled me forward.

My confidence and belief in what I was becoming and the person I so wanted to be was strong. I was comfortable with who I was. What's really interesting is that I was told without a university degree I was never going to succeed in business in Asia because I'd never get hired without a work visa.

My paradigm kicked in here too and I operated on a level as if I were educated with a university degree. I was spending time with people who had MBAs, degrees and high paid jobs. All my friends were successful business people and I had forgotten after a while that I didn't have a university degree. This became my world and on an unconscious level I was creating the movie of my life and changing my paradigms without even realizing it. It's so true that you are the sum person of the people that you spend the most time with.

I did end up finally achieving my ideal weight and size. The amazing part about this is that I didn't go into the "oh God I need to lose weight" mindset nor did I obsess over dieting. I am a foodie and I truly believe that food/wine is part of the "joie de vivre" that brings pure joy and happiness. Instead of eliminating one of my greatest passions, I decided to improve my relationship with food. I exercise to enjoy food and wine where I want, when I want and as much as I want. Since achieving my ideal size/weight at the age of 34, I have successfully maintained my physical health until today.

I was an unconscious competent – I didn't know what I was doing on a conscious level. I realise that now. But many people aren't and don't know what they have to do to make changes. Teaching people to really understand how their mind works is the absolute key and my life purpose. And to really help others you have to go through that transformation yourself. You can change your self-image. Just act like the person you want to become.

Obstacles

I started in fitness and administration then went into international relocation and corporate sales. My clients were in human resources and expats moving in and out of Asia. We got to teach them how to do business in Asia. I did the whole relocation executive package. That's when I moved up the corporate ladder and how I built my career.

I wasn't one who saved money or invested either. I believed in spending to make money. I am the classic unconscious competent. I had no clue on this level what I was doing I was just going intuitively. I conquered a lot of fears in Asia. I'm Chinese, I was born in Canada and had to face a whole society of girls that were so focused on how they looked and how skinny they were. In Asia everyone would ask, "Why are you so fat?" and every day I was ridiculed for not speaking Chinese. In Hong Kong there's a specific Chinese culture in itself. It was brutal.

From this job I went into sales and then I changed industries and I took pay cuts to take my career to the right level because I knew sales was where the money was and I was good at it. My personality is geared to business development. Even though I hated sales and networking, I loved connecting people. Interesting isn't it. I just had to get over these perceptions that I had and make a decision to do whatever it took to get me to where I want to go. This meant facing lots of fears and doing things that I didn't really enjoy.

I also had to find my own worthiness in relationship with men because when I was in a relationship I completely dominated. This was something I had to be really conscious about. I needed to be softer in all areas of my life because I knew I could be dominating on a daily basis.

I also didn't trust myself because I did things that were not trust-worthy. I had to work on being trustworthy. I guess that's the self-discovery in my twenties of taking a lot of risks. I really took a lot of risks but they weren't always conscious. The philosophy I live by is that I don't need to know everything or anything before I take action. I don't suffer very much from analysis paralysis. I just take action when I feel it's right without over-thinking it. I've been in situations where it may have been dangerous, in hindsight, but not knowing enabled me to proceed in life without unnecessary fears.

I am not someone who has to read everything. I wasn't in the self-development realm in that sense. I just intuitively knew what I needed to do for me.

Taking action

Friends over the years who are big in the self-help/personal development industry, would say, "Susan you have to read this book. You've got to watch this program." I was thinking to myself *if you tell me to read another book I'll explode.* I have 100 books in a pile that I haven't even touched yet.

I am just purely what I call a classic action figure.

I don't even think sometimes I just act. I found that the more I knew the less I did. The more I knew, the more I would think and the more it would delay me. I guess this might be a personal thing that all my learning was done through my own actions and most of the time it was unconsciously.

I'll give you an example. A previous boyfriend of mine was a big reader. He was one of those people who had to read "The Lonely Planet" for every single place he went before he got there. We were travelling to China and he was encouraging me to read too.

I wasn't interested in reading. I told him we'd just go there and see what happens. I was probably about 28 and we went to this stone forest. It was great and we went off the beaten path because there were just too many travelers with cameras.

Afterwards we went back to our hotel and he decided to open "The Lonely Planet" where he read that you should never go off the beaten path because there are people who'll rob you and kill you. We had a great time that day and experienced so many things that we wouldn't have if we had read that book. We can read things, and listen to other people's opinions and create limitations for ourselves rather than asking ourselves what we want, taking action and enjoying the experience. I'm not saying that everybody should do this, but it does cause you to experience more.

You need to be connected to yourself enough that you know when you're making the right decision and taking action.

People get into a lot of trouble is when they have too many filters in terms of information. This stops them from taking action. They have all this acquired knowledge which is toxic at this point because it creates fear and they can't move forward. They become paralyzed and procrastinate.

I went to the other side of the spectrum and just took action.

I knew that is who I was and I was never going to change that because I got results.

Money

Money does not motivate me. Interesting when we are focusing on becoming a millionaire, isn't it? Helping people connect is what motivates me. This might sound like the craziest thing, but I found that by helping more people, the money followed.

Relationships have always been my thing ever since I was young.

I think it was because my father programmed into me from a young age, "It's not what you know, it's who you know." My paradigms were purely tied to money where you have to work hard for your money. My parents worked 365 days a year in their restaurant. They never closed and always struggled to make money.

My father had spending and debt issues. He had debt all his life. Even today when he doesn't need to have debt, he keeps that debt. It's the programming. He just can't get out of it. I got him to lower his debt. I made him understand consciously, but subconsciously he ran up that debt again because he needed to have that debt. It was in harmony with his paradigm.

I lived in an environment where money and struggle went hand in hand. Thankfully I worked on myself, sought advice and created my own wealth.

I also learned that money is easy to come by. I remember when my dad gave me my first credit card. I was 14 and it had a $2,000 limit. That was 30-something years ago, so it was a large amount. I maxed it out in one week. It was always paid off because somebody would pay it off for me, either my boyfriend or my dad. It wasn't a positive, but it was a belief that money will always come somehow from somebody else.

My beliefs around money are quite different than others: that it's always easy to come by and that you know you always have it. I still spend a lot and I still make a lot.

When I got married, it changed a lot of things and how I operated. I had to work with somebody else's paradigms. At the time I didn't know what paradigms were. I had to work with somebody else's limiting beliefs around money and that was probably the most challenging thing in our relationship. That was another journey in itself.

Relationships

I believe we're supposed to work in conjunction with one another in this world so we never have to stand-alone.

To impact the world, we're meant to help each other. It's why I went into working with people, helping them to communicate better. When I was sales coaching all my coaching revolved around life coaching because I had to get my clients out of their own way. It's not a matter of teaching people how to sell, they knew how to sell. People had been in sales for years and years. All my coaching and my meeting with sales people was to help them develop relationships and really help people.

Retirement

When I retired from the bank at 46, I thought, "What am I going to do now?" I started my own coaching business full time, but I struggled for a year.

I felt awful charging people because I had gone so long not charging. I wasn't suffering because I knew when I didn't charge somebody, I got the money back from another area. I had to switch that paradigm. I started to change the paradigm of earning other people's money. Now it was time to earn myself money. Here I was in my 40s just making that decision.

Daily Success Habit

My most important success habit each and every day is visualisation. It's huge for me. I visualise my day and how it's going to be. If I have a meeting with a client, I visualise the outcome I want in my mind. I play this imaginary movie in my head in the morning and see the successful outcome I desire.

My mind is so powerful when I apply this. I just make a decision about the outcome that I want and it generally plays out that way.

Super Action Hero

I've been gifted the ability to be very aware of people. Everybody has a certain quality that I admire. I always look at the quality and weigh up whether or not it would serve me. If I liked that quality and thought it would improve me, I add it to my own qualities. I call it creating my own super action hero. The best version of myself which I can always improve upon.

Mentor

One thing I wish I had known about when I was younger is the importance of having a mentor. I think all young people need to know that there's a way to help our thinking and our results. In society today, I think it's way more important than people think it is.

I believe if I had had a mentor, it would have halved the time for me to become a self-made millionaire. Having a mentor who has done what you want to do quickens the process.

Susan's Key Ingredients to Success

Firstly, be an action taker all the time. This is the absolute key. Always take action. Make a decision, take action fast. Your answers, people, resources and opportunities will come when you keep doing that.

Secondly, always know what you want. Always keep focused on what you want whether it's a job, a business or an opportunity that fits you.

Thirdly know who you are. Really get to know who you are, the good and bad. Work out the things that are serving you and get rid of the things that aren't. Figure out what else you need and make that part of your super action hero self-image.

Convince yourself that an intellect has nothing to do with success.

Just because somebody knows a lot doesn't mean that they're taking action and applying it. Be an action taker.

SUMMARY

- Take action
- Get to know yourself and change what isn't serving you
- Develop confidence
- Make a decision to go after what you want
- Conquer fears

CHAPTER 3 | BOB PROCTOR

Bob made his first million before he was 30. Bob is my mentor and what I have learned from him has completely changed my life and the lives of the clients I work with. He's been a legendary figure in the world of personal development for over 57 years. Bob has been the inspiration for millions of people and businesses worldwide to create million dollar fortunes.

As I write this book, Bob is 84 and presenting seminars worldwide, developing programs and incredibly inspired to share this information with as many people possible.

Developing Your Mindset and Your Success

I've been in the personal development business since 1968 and studying since 1961. Most people think it's the study and the programs that make the changes, but you have to get out there and do it.

The key factor that contributed to my mindset and success was reading Napoleon Hill's book, "Think and Grow Rich" every day. I've been reading this book and studying it every day for 57 years.

This book is really the thinking of 500 of the world's greatest thinkers and greatest wealth accumulators between 1900 and 1935. The book came out in 1937 and Napoleon studied the lives of Henry Ford, Rockerfeller, Thomas Edison, Harvey Firestone, you name it. Real and very accomplished individuals. He studied them for years and found there was a golden thread running through their lives. Although they were in many different fields, they had similar ways of looking at things. Their thinking and perception of things were similar.

The books I've read, the recordings I've listened to and the people who have mentored me, have been largely responsible for the way I see the world and the way I work.

But the key is taking action on what you read and listen to, and making sure this action in alignment with your goal.

Everybody's mind is set. What you want to do is take a look at the results you're getting. This will tell you where your mind is set.

It's like looking at the thermometer in a house. When you want to find out what the temperature of the house is, you go and check out the thermostat. If you want to check out the temperature of your body, you put the thermometer under your tongue. If you want to check out the temperature of your life or your mindset, you take a look at your results. The problem with most people is that they look at the results but they don't understand that the results are a measurement of what's going on in their mind.

People want to blame something or someone outside of themselves, rather than taking responsibility for themselves.

Over a long period of reading and studying, my life changed. You just can't read, watch and listen, you do have to act. I read many years ago, it said no amount of reading or memorizing is going to make a person successful in life. It's the understanding and application of wise thoughts that count. The application has to be there.

Learning is when we consciously entertain it. We get emotionally involved. We step and act on it and we change the end result.

It's the feedback from the change in result that is the learning experience. We're on the track where we think the trick is if we read the book and we can answer questions about the content of the book correctly, then we've learned it.

That's not true at all. This means you have gathered the information, possibly remembered it, but it doesn't mean you have learned it. That's the path school puts us on because that's the way our organized education system works. People have the wrong idea with respect to learning anything. Learning is not just gathering the information and being able to repeat it or answer the questions correctly. It's acting on the ideas and changing the end result.

If I take an idea and I think about it, I get emotionally involved in it, which I have to do if I'm going to act on it, Then, I step out and act on the idea. I see whether that idea works or not by the results I'm getting. It's the feedback from the results. Then I can determine whether or not it's a good idea, whether it worked.

Authors Note: Hearing that education is located in the conscious mind was a very pivotal point in my life. I finally understood that my paradigms (located in the subconscious mind) were limiting my success. I made the decision to share this with as many people as I could.

Beliefs and Self-Image

The beliefs I had about myself since I started to study and now have changed dramatically. I had very little belief in myself. I had a very poor image of myself. I had done nothing to improve it and my environment did nothing to improve it.

Keep in mind I was born during a depression. I spent my young life between birth and 12 years old either in a depression or a world war where everything was rationed. There were very few parents at home. Most of the ones in my neighborhood were in Europe or the Pacific fighting. The parents were working in war factories.

My grandmother raised me. There wasn't much time given to making sure that children's minds were raised right. I mean the idea was for children to have enough to eat, were they warm, were they properly clothed?

The idea of developing the mind of a person was not even a consideration.

At a very young age I developed the self-image that I had of myself. Of course, it wasn't very good. I did poorly at school. I wasn't interested in learning and the school said that was my fault and I don't pay attention.

I found out later that it's the teacher's responsibility to get the child's attention, hold their attention and get them emotionally involved in the information.

That wasn't part of the game back then. They didn't understand that. I don't blame them, they did the best they could. I did the best under the circumstances, but I didn't learn much.

When I left school at 15 or 16 to go to work, I had very little to offer.

We go to work to sell our time, our energy, our loyalty and our knowledge to a company and they are going to pay us well for that.

I didn't have much to offer, so I never got much.

I went into the navy at a very young age. When I came out, I worked in bars and factories and then I became a fireman. That was my life. I was spending more than I earned, and living a life of lack and limitation.

That went on until I met someone who told me I could have anything I wanted. I didn't believe that, but I believed he believed it and that got my attention. That's when my life started changing at 26 years of age. He gave me information to study. He gave me direction and everything started to change just like that.

I became so fascinated with the information that I've never stopped studying. If you study something for a long time, you're going to learn something about it and that's what I've done.

Having a healthy self-image is important to success in all areas of your life. It's absolutely essential.

If you can't see yourself doing something well, you're not going to do it well. If you can't see yourself building something, you're not going to build it. I don't care what it is. I don't care if it is a sand castle on the beach, you have to see the result in your mind. If you're getting dressed to go somewhere, you see yourself with what you're going to wear, so you go and put those clothes on.

Maxwell Maltz discovered that you have two images of yourself and wrote a book on it called *Psychocybernetics* in 1960. It was considered one of the greatest psychological breakthroughs of his generation. He was a cosmetic surgeon and he would operate on a person and maybe remove a very distasteful scare from your face or do a nose job. He found sometimes there was not only a physical change, but there was a great psychological change of the person after the operation. In contrast, sometimes he'd make a great physical change and it would look tremendous, but there was no psychological change in the patient.

That made him postulate that we might have two images. There's one that comes back from the mirror, but then we've got this one on the inside. Quite often the one that comes back from the mirror is very different from inside.

You see a very good-looking young woman and she won't look you in the eye. She's always looking down. She slouches when she walks. That person is physically quite attractive, but mentally she doesn't think so. It's the same with a man. I remember a cousin of mine. She was just a stunning looking young lady. If she had a little zit on her face, all her attention went to the zit, she didn't look at the beauty.

Some people are programmed to look at what's wrong instead of what's right. That's how the self-image works. The more we learn about ourselves, the more fascinated we'll become. I'm not suggesting a person should become conceited, because that's is on the wrong track. I think they should have a real healthy respect for who they are.

The more they study themselves, the more they are going to have a healthy respect.

When you study the body, the physical aspects and the composition of the body it's mind-boggling. If you only study the blood, it's fascinating. Blood circulates through hundreds of miles of passageway every 33 seconds, and it carries all the food in and all the garbage out in one sweeping change.

Study the brain. It's an electronic switching station and it controls the vibration of this massive station we call the body. When we activate different brain cells, the body moves into different vibrations. As it does, it adds and attracts all kinds of different stuff. You can study the emotional aspect, the spiritual side, or the intellectual side of us. We live simultaneously on three planes. We have an intellect, we are spiritual beings and we live in a physical body.

The more you study this, the more you get blown away with who you are, what you are capable of and your self-image starts to improve.

A good, healthy self-image is essential. Everyone has a self-image, but not everyone has a good one. If you want to see a person with a good self-image, take a look at their life. Their self-image is expressed in the results showing up in their lives.

Paradigms and Programming

You see, the self-image is only one aspect of what we're really talking about. It really comes down to how a person is programmed.

We're programmed at birth. We're programmed genetically which is why we look like our relatives. The influences of our genetic pool goes back for generations and is built right into our genes.

When I was a young man, I had red hair. I have a brother and a sister, neither of them had red hair. My mother and father didn't have red hair. Now this could have led to all kinds of speculation, but my mother's father and all his brothers had red hair.

Sometimes these similarities in our genetic likeness or nature go back – one, two or more generations. You'll find mixed races where two white people are giving birth to a dark baby because somewhere in that genetic strain there was a mixed marriage and so it comes out. That's in our DNA, in our genetic conditioning.

You have to stop at first and say where did that come from? A little particle of energy from mum and a little particle of dad came together. It resonated. It was in harmony and that formed a little piece of you. Two-hundred eighty days later you made your debut on the planet.

Well where did mum come from? Where did dad come from? This takes you back into the grandparents on both sides. Where did they come from? And then you're into the great grandparents on both sides. Well, you're the combination of that genetic pool. At the moment of conception, the genetics began.

When you're born, your subconscious mind is wide open. Your subconscious mind is totally deductive. It has no ability to reject information. It will accept anything that goes into it. Which is precisely why almost all welfare recipients are third, fourth and fifth generation welfare recipients. They are genetically programmed for it and then their environment reinforces it as well.

The programming continues on in their little life until they are about five or six years old, until they start to think for themselves. The odds of a person breaking out of this used to be rather slim. The odds of today are much greater because there's all kinds of information that has helped us understand how this programming has taken place and how to change it, which is precisely what you are doing by sharing this book with readers.

All that programming is the paradigm. The paradigm is nothing but an idea or a multitude of ideas that have been fixed in the subconscious mind. A habit is something that's fixed in the subconscious mind that automatically expresses itself without any conscious thought. You put your makeup on by habit. You comb your hair by habit. You get dressed by habit. You don't have to think, you can be thinking of all kinds of things while you're getting dressed. You can be thinking of all kinds of things while you're eating. This is habitual behaviour.

Almost all of our behaviour is habitual. The paradigm is really controlling us. We have got to stop and say, "Wait a minute what am I doing? What do I believe about me?" If you analyse your beliefs in light of truth, you're going to realise that most of your beliefs are absurd. They are absolutely ridiculous.

You're controlled by two powers, either religion or science. They are the only sources of reference we have to go to.

Now, we're told that we're created in the image of God and I believe that. The problem is that we reversed that. We created God in our image. That's where the confusion started. We started to see a man on a cloud, not a woman, a man, and we say that's God. When we do this, we go down the road in sheer fantasy.

We are taught by every religion. I don't care which one. You can be Baptist or Protestant. You could be Catholic or you could be Hindu, Jewish, or Hebrew. You could be any of them, it doesn't matter. They all teach one God. One plan. One power. If you go to science, they tell you it's all energy. Religion tells you its Spirit. They use different names for the same thing.

That's what we're an expression of. They say that God is all powerful. If we are created in the image of God, then we are all powerful. We say God is all knowing. If God is all knowing, then we must be all knowing. God is present. He can be present in all places at all times. When you refer to science, they say everything is energy. This computer is energy. The pen I use is energy. My body is energy. My hair is energy. This book is energy. The air is energy, everything is energy.

They say God is all knowledge and all the power and it's all in the present. This means it's within me. This doesn't mean that I am God. I have been created in that energy.

We have been given powers and facilities beyond the scope of our imagination. All the little creatures on the planet, the kangaroos, the dog, the duck, the squirrel, any animal, they blend in and are completely at home in their environment. You and I are totally disoriented within our environment and that's because we have been give these God-like facilities. These higher facilities to create our own environment. The image that we hold of ourselves is going to dictate how we do it.

If I think I can't do that very well, I'm not going to do it very well. But if I think I can do that really well, I can do a tremendous job, all I have to do is learn it. And I can learn anything if I make up my mind. This is the link with your self-image.

Money

I didn't have any money and I was like most people. I wanted to earn some money. I applied what I learned.

Ray Stanford, the man I was talking to, had all kinds of money. He was happy, healthy and wealthy. The carrot he dangled in front of me to make money was very attractive.

He pointed out to me that my way of doing things wasn't working and said, "Why don't you try mine." That seemed to make sense. I guess I didn't have a lot going for me, but what he said made sense. Why would I continue doing what I was doing, getting the results I was getting, when I could take advice from someone who was happy, healthy and wealthy?

I started listening to him and doing what he told me to do. He gave me the book and told me to study that, and he kept telling me the ideas to act on.

I told him I didn't know how to earn money. He said, "You earn money by providing a service. Do anything."

Somebody said to me, "There's good money in cleaning floors." I didn't have a problem with that, so I started cleaning floors and that is where I started.

I was getting great direction, and I guess I was awake enough to follow it.

You see, I was following it because I really wanted the money. And the money started coming in.

I had a goal of earning $25,000 per year. I didn't really believe that I could do that. I didn't even know anyone with $25,000 except the guy that was giving me advice.

Money is a reward that you receive for service rendered. If you provide a little bit of service, you only get a little bit of money. Now I started cleaning floors and Ray said, "You can earn a lot of money cleaning floors. He said "You can earn a lot of money at anything."

He didn't tell me what to work at, he just told me to go to work.

And when you go to work you provide service.

He said, "If you're working for yourself, then you make the rules so that's what I recommend you do. I followed his advice.

I got one office to clean, then I got another and another. I got to the point where I couldn't clean any more offices. I thought the answer was to clean another office. I literally passed out on the street from sheer exhaustion. I mean I was working so hard. I wasn't sleeping properly. I wasn't eating.

I woke up one day on the street and there was a great big police officer looking at me. I saw a crowd of people around me and lights flashing, it was a scary situation. I finally talked them out of taking me to the hospital. They had a stretcher there and everything. I think somebody thought I had dropped dead.

I sat down and I got thinking about it what had just happened.

I realised I was doing something wrong.

And a little voice in my head said, "If you can't clean all of them, don't clean any of them." I thought that was good advice to give myself.

That's when I got other people cleaning for me. I got all dressed up. I got a shirt and tie on and I got other people cleaning offices.

In less than five years, I was cleaning offices in Toronto, Montreal, Boston, Cleveland, Atlanta, and London, England. I would've kept on going if I hadn't fallen on the information I teach today.

But one day I realised, this is what I wanted to do. The secret was I directed energy. I multiplied what I was doing and that's what you've got to do.

I leveraged myself.

You can only apply so much service and time yourself. You trade your time for money when you are doing it yourself and you run out of time. I don't know how many people I had cleaning offices. I had all kinds of people cleaning that I didn't even know personally. I got managers in the offices and I got supervisors on the road.

I didn't learn this in school, I just did it. And it worked.

I believe that my idea of money is the same as most people's.

I believed that people who earned money were lucky. I believed I'd never have any money. I believed that I'd always be short of money. I believed that I couldn't earn a lot of money. I wouldn't even apply for a job where you could earn a lot of money. I had ridiculous ideas about money, absolutely absurd.

As I started to learn about money, I became absolutely fascinated with it. Now, there's a very strong caution here. A lot of people let money control them and then they're in real trouble. You've go to control money. Money makes a wonderful servant, but it makes a terrible master.

In my book, "Born Rich," I said you should love people and use money and I have lived by that. I will not let money control me.

I love to earn it. I love setting money as a goal because I can measure it straight to the penny. I know exactly how well l am doing, however, I won't let it control me. I just absolutely refuse to.

Now money is a reward we seek for service rendered.

There are three strategies when it comes to earning money.

The number one is a strategy that 95% of people use. They trade their time for money. That is an inherent problem it's called saturation. Why? There are only 24 hours in a day and you can run out of time.

The number two strategy is that you invest money to earn money. This is a great strategy and if you're good at it, you can do very well. You can put your money to work for you. You can take a bit of money and buy real estate or invest in stocks. This is where your money is working for you. You can invest in all kinds of ways but you have to be good at it.

The third strategy is to multiply your time by setting up multiple sources of income. You can set up sources of income all over the world, and there's no end to how much you can earn. You put the money to work here, there everywhere and you have access globally.

I see money as an instrument that allows me to provide services far beyond my own physical presence.

I give a lot of money away. I understand the law. The more you give, the more you receive. I don't give to receive. I give it to give. You have to give for the right reason. You've got to really enjoy letting it go. You should never let money own you.

I just decide on a number and I go and earn it and I keep raising the bar, so I keep earning more. I was earning $4,000 a year and I owed $6,000 when I started. Today I earn millions of dollars and I intend to earn millions more. But it doesn't make me a better person. It makes me what I already am. Fortunately, I was raised by a mother who was very generous. She didn't have much but she shared what she had, and that's how I live.

Authors Note: Bob shares this beautiful story about his mother as a memory from his childhood and it's such a great reminder to be a generous giver.

I was probably 12 and it was a very cold winter. We heated the houses with coal furnaces to keep warm and the coal truck would come and dump the coal into a window in the basement. It was a dirty way to heat the house, but it was effective and that's what everybody used.

There was a family that lived on the next street and the kids went to our school. They didn't have any coal, so they were cold. One of the kids was in my class and I came home and told my mother about it. She got a twenty dollar bill, which was a lot of money back then, and sent us to the store to break it for two tens. She gave me one ten and asked me to take it to this boys' mother and give it to her to buy a ton of coal. She didn't even know the family. Now that was 72 years ago and here I am sharing it with you. It left an impression on my mind that has never gone.

Work Smarter Not Harder

Many people who are in business don't leverage themselves. They are trading their time for money. They might as well have a job. They're working more in their business than they probably should.

Michael Gerber says, "If your business requires your presence, you don't have a business, you have a job." He says that a lot of people have what you call an entrepreneurial seizure. They don't like their job. They don't like their boss, so they're going to work for themselves and they aren't a very good boss sometimes.

They don't have enough awareness of how to do things.

So, what they've really done is trade one job for another, and trade one boss for another. They're not doing it right. They don't have a business, they actually have a job, they just think they have a business.

The key is leveraging and being able to provide more service to more people.

Mentors

I think mentors are essential. Too often people ask somebody for help and too often this person doesn't know any more than they do. They say, "Would you help me with this," but they don't know how. We should go to people who've already demonstrated results because they know what they're doing, instead of just picking someone at random.

I'm probably a mentor to millions, certainly thousands, through the recordings that I put out on Youtube.com and the courses we offer. You can have a mentor who you really spend a fare amount of time with and be sure you choose someone that has already done what you want to do.

I really credit most of the success I've enjoyed to the mentors I've had. I've done the work. They told me what to do; recommended what to read; what to study and I had great direction. I think we need direction. We need guidance and I think the guides you choose are very important. Choose people to mentor you who have already demonstrated their results because they know what they're doing.

My first mentor was Ray Stanford, the man that gave me the "Think and Grow Rich" book. He said to me, "Listen your way's not working, Bob. Why don't you try mine? If you do exactly what I tell you, I am going to show you how to win." He'd say, "Just do what I tell you to until you find out that I'm lying or that I don't know what I'm talking about."

Well, he didn't lie and he did know what he was talking about.

And for whatever reason, I just kept doing what he said. I used this as a yard stick.

Are they telling me the truth?

If somebody tells you the truth, you'll know it. That's because it resonates with the essence of who you are. There is perfection within you and so that resonates at the same frequency as the essence of who you are. I know when people are telling the truth and when they're lying too. I tested Ray. I would do what he said and then I'd find out he was telling me the truth. I've had about six or seven mentors and that was the litmus test

I tell people to do that with me.

I say, "Do exactly what I tell you. I mean don't try and study so you know as much as I do about it. First of all, you don't need to know, because a lot of what I know is useless information. Some of it is very effective. Do exactly what I tell you until you find out if I am lying to you."

I'm not going to lie to you and I do know what I am talking about.

I'm considered an international expert on this subject, which I always find rather interesting because all I've done is just taken some simple material and applied it in my life based upon what my mentors suggested.

Challenges and Obstacles

Overcoming challenges and obstacles is necessary for your growth. Most people don't understand this and will stay in their comfort zones. Fear is caused by ignorance and you're always going where you've never been if you're growing. Your setting goals to do things that you've never done. It can be scary and uncomfortable.

That's where faith comes in and you have just got to have faith that you can do it.

Faith is the ability to see the invisible, to believe in the incredible. Seeing yourself doing something you've never done before, but you really see yourself doing it in your mind.

It's incredible to believe that I can create an image in my mind just out of pure nothing. Pure spirit or energy. I can create an image in my conscious mind, and if I impress that image upon my subconscious mind, my subconscious mind has no ability to reject it. It's totally deductive. It has no ability to reject. It will accept it as real and then it will control the vibration and so it will control my actions.

Faith is the ability to see the invisible, believe in the incredible and that will cause you to receive what the masses call impossible.

The more faith you have in the spirit of yourself, and work with it, the more you are going to accomplish.

I go into areas I have never been and I start doing things I've never done and sometimes I make mistakes.

I had the idea to do a seminar on a cruise in the South Seas. I decided we would rent a ship, sell tickets and have guest speakers come on the cruise. It was very successful and we earned about one hundred thousand dollars in profit. (Which wasn't a lot for the week because it cost us a lot to run the company but everybody had a great time and we still earned a profit).

The next year we decided to do it again. We got a much bigger ship. The outcome was we lost two million dollars and I don't do cruises anymore!

I found out what I didn't know and that was you should stick to what you know. You shouldn't go into a business that you don't understand. We did that. We didn't understand and lost a lot of money.

Now when that happens, it's a learning experience. Do you let it bother you? I didn't let it bother me at all that I had made a mistake.

You see, you don't learn from your wins, you learn from your losses and when you understand that, you lose the fear of losing and you just get out there and do it.

I'm not afraid to try anything. It scares the daylights out of me sometimes, but I go ahead and do it anyway. I know what's causing the fear. I just understand it. I know if I keep edging into it, my understanding develops and very soon I'm not afraid of it at all.

And that is how we grow. If we let fear stop us we live a limited life.

Worry and doubt come from ignorance, and understanding comes from knowledge. Solomon said, "In all you are getting, get understanding." He was a very knowledgeable guy. There's only one way to get understanding. It's to study. There's no other way. There are many forms of study, the book you are preparing. That's going to help a lot of people as they study it. Understanding is the opposite to doubt and fear, they are polar opposites.

I don't live with doubt and fear. Understand what is causing the fear. Understand the laws of the universe. Understand the laws of creation. Understand the creative processes locked up inside of yourself. Understanding is the key to everything and understanding leads to faith.

Daily Success Habits

There is a success habit I have every day - when I wake up, I get up. I don't press the snooze button; I get out of bed and I make things happen. I'm always productive. I want to be involved in goal achieving activities all the time. I don't have a lot of spare time. I was reading where Napoleon Hill was interviewing Andrew Carnegie way back in 1903, something like that, and he asked Carnegie what he did with his spare time. Carnegie said, "I don't have any spare time." That made a very strong impression on me.

I have a little spare time, but I don't have a lot of spare time. I keep myself booked very tight.

I get up most mornings at 5 am and go out into my studio and study. I study for an hour, sometimes more. I'm a very productive individual.

I delegate a lot of work to other people. I do what I'm really good at and stay away from what I'm not good at. I think everybody needs an assistant. If anybody wants to be successful, you need an assistant. Gina keeps my calendar she has been with me for over thirty years and she's an excellent assistant.

Recipe for Success

First of all, you have to understand what success is. I think Earl Nightingale's definition for success is as good as you are going to find anywhere. He said, "Success is the progressive realization of a worthy ideal." It's progressive. You have to keep moving toward it progressively. You don't stop and start. You progressively move toward it. It's the progressive realisation that you're becoming more aware of a worthy idea. It has to be worthy of you. You don't ask if you are worthy of it. It has got to be worthy of you

If you're going to dedicate your life to something, you want to make it really worthwhile, so it has to be a worthy ideal. An ideal is an idea that we are in love with, that you really resonate with. Love is when your intellect, emotion and physical being are locked into the idea. That is love. When two people are in love they are connected intellectually, emotionally and physically. Most people get connected physically. They have sex and think they're in love. They're not in love at all. They're having fun. Love is when you are really connected to a person. Intellectually your ideas have a rapport, your emotions have a rapport and then you have a physical relationship, that's love. You can fall in love with an idea. This happens when intellectually, emotionally and physically you're in harmony with it. Success is the progressive realisation that you are moving towards. Become more aware of an ideal that is worthy of you. Worthy of sharing and trading your life for. An idea that you are in love with. I think it's a perfect definition and recipe for success.

One Thing I Wish I'd Known

I would've liked to know about the God-given power that we have locked up within us. The absolute magnificence of our mind.

That's why I think every parent needs to understand it, so they can give it to their children. If you can get it across to kids, there's no end to where they can go.

You can teach children to read before they can talk. We teach them languages, we teach them multiple languages. I had an associate in Kuala Lumpur, Malaysia. He had a four-year-old boy who spoke four languages and they thought nothing of it. He could speak more than four languages because that what was spoken to him and he didn't think it was out of the ordinary.

We don't know what a child is capable of learning and we teach them very slowly, and we teach them in packs all together. It's absurd that we think they're going to all learn at the same speed. Eighty percent of people have never done what they are teaching, so the fact that we are making progress is pretty amazing.

If I was starting over, I'd start studying seriously at a very early age, knowing what I know. I believe we could spend all of our lives seriously studying, but you have got to act on it. No-one really knows what we're capable of doing. I have accomplished relatively nothing compared to what I'm capable of doing. I'm always trying to do more, be more.

SUMMARY

- Take action
- You earn money by providing a service
- Work smarter not harder
- Be generous with your giving
- Choose people to mentor you who have already done what you want to do
- Success is the progressive realization of a worthy ideal

Bob's Suggested Reading

Think and Grow Rich, Napoleon Hill

How to raise yourself from failure to success, Frank Betteger

Chapter IV *Principal of Guidance, Hidden Power*, Thomas Troward

Chapter XI *Touching Lightly, Hidden Power*, Thomas Troward

Chapter XVIII *Entering into the Spirit of it, Hidden Power*, Thomas Troward

Psycho-Cybernetics, Maxwell Maltz

CHAPTER 4 | JACKIE CARROLL

Currently: Founder of GIAH International

Jackie lives in Ireland and made her first million when she was 28. Her goal now is to help over a billion people create and manifest their dreams through visualisation using Genie in a handset (GIAH). Specific moments in Jackie's life shaped decisions for her future resilience. She has a burning desire to create more for her life and bring happiness and joy wherever she goes. Jackie wanted more. She knew that she was more than capable of doing more, but her self-image and money paradigm were preventing her success. Once she made these changes, the success quickly followed. Hers is an inspirational story of that inner knowing that the best is yet to come.

"If you can live with a dream in your head, hope in your heart and a smile on your face, you will have a lot more than most."

Background

I was born in Zimbabwe and grew up in South Africa. Now I live in Ireland. When I separated from my previous partner, my family were living in Ireland so I moved there in 2003 and married.

Life-Shaping Events

When I was a teenager, my dad had been working for a company for about 15 years and was quite a dedicated employee. I think the company saw more of him than we did growing up, and out of the blue one day he was just retrenched.

This was an emotional impact for me because how could a big corporation that you dedicated so much of your time to over the years, just let you go? Like you were dispensable?

It really affected me on a deep level. I remember he was really hurt and upset by it. I thought to myself that is never going to happen to me.

From that day on I decided I was going to be this amazing businessperson, and I was going to have my own company. I was going to have employees and was never going to let that happen to anyone else. This was my first lesson in being the master of my own destiny.

Fast forward a few years and I was always holding onto the idea of being my own boss. I got into the film industry. My dream was to have my own production company and whatever industry I got into I was always reaching for more. Wanting to be the owner and not just an employee. I was never satisfied with what I had and I always wanted to have more. It was a burning desire within me.

When I was 19, my mum passed with cancer a week before my 20th birthday, and that was another turning point in my life. I think that was ultimately when I discovered what my life purpose was going to be. It was just over a month between her diagnosis and her passing. It was so quick. She died very unhappy. It was like she had given up on life. All her hope had abandoned her. She had given up on her dreams and her life. Essentially, I think that's why she died so quickly. I know that some of my family might not agree with me, but that's what I thought and felt. We were very close and I could see she was very unhappy. It affected me deeply.

I don't think that anyone should die giving up their dreams or having no hope left.

That was where my desire to live came from. My little saying in life is. "If you can live with a dream in your head, hope in your heart and a smile on your face, you'll have a lot more than most."

Being appreciative and grateful for what we have is important to me. Essentially, I feel that my life's purpose is to give people that hope to allow them to dream again.

If they do that, they can fall in love with life again.

People shouldn't fall out of love with life, they should be constantly in love as if they have a savage love affair with life. People always comment that I'm always smiling and always happy. I just love life so much and choose to enjoy it.

Money

Our beliefs around money growing up were the usual things. We can't afford, it we don't have enough, money doesn't grow on trees, the usual sayings. We grew up with the paradigm operating from lack instead of abundance.

Before I made the shift, I was brought up with the belief that "I'm not Rockefeller I'm the other feller." I still felt there was more and there was always that longing. I kept thinking, this can't be it. I know I'm destined for more.

Developing a healthier self-image allowed me to attract more money.

Focusing on my goal, building my confidence, fueling my desire and focusing on changing my money paradigm changed everything for me.

If I didn't believe in who I was and what I was doing I wouldn't have gotten very far.

It's also important to have the desire for a particular goal that you're reaching for. It also works in reverse. You can have the self-confidence and the self-image, but if you don't have the desire to be more, do more, want more, nothing will change. If you don't have the desire around it, you're not going to do what it takes to make it happen.

Even though I had the self-confidence to always push through, I would never have attracted the investors I have currently if I didn't have the burning desire. I had no idea where the money was going to come from to make my dream a reality, I just had no idea how I was going to make it happen. But I kept focusing on my goal and working on my self-belief.

Obstacles

When my husband Shane and I got together he taught me a lot about property and we invested in a couple of commercial properties, flipped them over and made a decent amount. I think I was 28 when we made our first million.

Then we decided to invest in a business in South Africa. We were there for two years and used everything. This was a lesson in its self, just trying to think what else we could do. We left South Africa and returned to Ireland. Essentially what we had wanted to do was to find a business, turn it into a cash cow and then sell it. It didn't work out like that. We lost everything and returned to Ireland with our tails between our legs. Everybody kept saying to us, "You're the unluckiest people we know. Everything that could go wrong is happening to you."

Unfortunately, we latched onto that mindset and literally everything just fell to the wayside. We lost everything. That's when I also lost custody of my first daughter.

I had to make the choice to leave my daughter and return to Ireland, as I was pregnant with my second daughter. This was a real low point, but the growth and strength I gained from this experience just made me stronger.

We returned to Ireland and started Shane's business, Goldbank; in 2010. His company is now very successful. He does gold and silver trading and is now stretching out into the diamond and jewelry market. After having my next two children and helping him with his business, I started thinking that I wanted and needed something for me.

I was attracted to network marketing. I would get some success and then it would all taper out. I tried another company and then another one. I thought it was the business I was in that wasn't doing well. I thought it wasn't the right product or wasn't the right compensation plan, because it wasn't taking off for me. But now I realise it was all in the mind. All of my paradigms were limiting me.

I saw all these people doing and achieving incredible things in these companies and I was thinking, "I can do this. There's nothing more special about them than there is about me." I can do exactly what they're doing. What the hell, what's going on? Why can't I get to where I want to go?"

I was at rock bottom and my friend Eric said told me I had to go to this event. I think he asked me three times to come and listen to a presentation. I made every excuse why I couldn't go. I think at that stage, my whole self-image had just crashed.

I wasn't in a great place and neither was my marriage. I was starting to pile on load and loads of weight I had started to eat a lot and was drinking lots of wine to dull my pain.

I was really unhappy. I felt so much pain on the inside. I'm so grateful that Eric kept asking me to go along. I was thinking to myself I've run out of excuses, I've got nothing else to lose. I went along and that's when everything changed for me.

This really led me into self-development and transforming my self-image through the Thinking into Results program. I had that desire in me that was longing for more.

Self-development Beliefs

Be the master of your own destiny is one of the beliefs that I've learned to live by. As I mentioned, I always wanted more, however I never felt I was enough. I felt like I always had to prove myself to people. I was looking for approval from everybody. What I lacked was belief and confidence in myself.

That was the one thing that was holding me back.

Even though I had all these big dreams and big aspirations, and I wanted my own everything, I was battling my paradigms. I had no idea how they were controlling my results.

I got a taste of self-development in South Africa when I decided to do a two week evening course run by Baruch Banai at the Insight Training Centre. I don't think I realised it, but looking back that was the first step I took into trying to grow my awareness and reach for more. Develop myself. I then moved to Ireland where I met my next mentor, Ewa Pietrzak. I went to one of her events and I remember sitting in that hotel room watching her talk, thinking is this the day that's going to change my life forever?

I will never forget that thought. It was quite amazing. I put two and two together and then it was like, *oh wow*.

I didn't apply myself the first time I did Thinking into Results, but I did get good results. I thought, if I didn't apply myself can you imagine what I would get if I do this again and apply myself 100%? The second time I applied myself and that's where the Genie In A Headset (GIAH) idea came from.

It was only when I really evaluated myself that I realised I was holding myself back. It was like *Wow, okay, I get it*.

I literally transformed myself. Just like the caterpillar transforms into a butterfly. I transformed and built my inner belief and confidence and that's when the world started to open up.

Confidence in yourself is so important.

And it wasn't just my personal self-image that had to transform, it was also my money self-image and my money paradigm.

I was kind of successful to a certain point, but then all my results would just stagnate and I'd fall back again. I'd think, "What the hell am I doing wrong I know that I'm worth more. I know I meant for better, but why can't I get there?"

I had dabbled in different businesses over the years. I wanted to be my own boss and told myself I'm going to enjoy what I do. I had started up my own children gymnastics business and that was giving me a basic average salary.

Due to family circumstances, I had to pass over the business. I gave the business to my dad to run. I had to find employment in a company job so I could keep my daughter because my business wasn't making enough money to show the courts that I could support her.

It was faith knowing that when you see the physical results around you as long as you believe the fact that it will come, you don't have to know how. It was faith, 100% faith, knowing that it was absolutely going to happen. Chapter 4 "Let Go and Let God" from Bob Proctor's book "You Were Born Rich" saved me so many times. Having faith changed everything it helped me to continue to believe in myself and my goal.

I started working for a company called First Level Ventures which was all about venture capital, investing in companies. Interestingly enough, when I look back and connect the dots this is what has happened for me where investors have invested in my idea. I had to go through this work "experience" to understand investor's minds in preparation for GIAH.

It just shows you how everything happens for a reason.

The Birth of a Dream

I see so many people around me who aren't happy and just need to make a change. People feel that they have to live like this and don't realise they have a choice.

This is why I invented GENIE IN A HEADSET.

Our slogan is "We are the crusader of your dreams."

Essentially that's what we are. We are crusaders for each and everybody's dreams out there. We want people to have those dreams again. We want people to live like children and live in their imagination, build and live beautiful lives. We all deserve it.

That's where I started, I suppose.

I started pursuing this dream about three years ago. I started pitching on Voom. Richard Branson has a competition where you can enter your business and I pitched there. I did a lot of other different pitches and it was only when I went to the MATRIXX last year that GIAH International was born. I met investors made contacts at the MATRIXX.

Bob Proctor introduced me to Shawn Mangano. Then Shawn introduced me to all these other amazing people that I made connections with and that's when GIAH was born. Now I'm turning my dream into a reality.

We're only a year old, but in that time, so many amazing things have happened. I've met so many incredible people. It's amazing that all the people, resources and opportunities show up when you're pursuing your dream. I've met with Tony Robbins, Gary Vaynerchuk and many others to share my product with them.

I've always been in and out of trying this and that and being pretty average. I was always wanting more. When I became a millionaire, I realised I could do more. I have now become a billionaire in my mind. It was last year, 2017, when GIAH was born. Investors backed my idea and I am only realizing now how big of an idea it really is.

Daily Success Habits

I wake up in the morning and make a gratitude list of everything I'm grateful for. Then I take five minutes for silence, asking for guidance. I set my intentions for the day and send love to people that bother me. If I don't have anyone bothering me, I just send love to everyone that I love anyway.

Then I spend some time writing in my journal. Things like: what my thoughts are and what I'm really excited about for the day. I stand in front of my vision board and read my self-image and purpose statements. It takes about half an hour to do all that. Then I do personal study as well. I'm currently studying the New Lead the Field program. I treat my study as a business appointment and schedule it into my calendar. I schedule all my work and things I need to do. At the end of the day, I write down six goal-achieving activities I need to get done for the next day. Before I go to sleep, I visualise and I do my affirmations in the mirror.

Get a Mentor

If you want to change your current results and don't know how to do it, find yourself a mentor, someone who is already where you want to be. You can always do it by yourself, but if you aren't guided by people who have done it, you get caught up in your existing results. You need a mentor, someone who's going to help you get from where you are to where you want to go, to give you clear focus, direction and help you get unstuck.

SUMMARY

- Have a very clear goal in mind
- Get yourself into a daily routine or daily habit of self-development
- Develop a healthy self-image
- Build your confidence
- Find the person that you want to be like. If it's a million you want to make, then find yourself a millionaire and get them to mentor you
- Love life and choose to enjoy it!

CHAPTER 5 | DEMO CASANOVA

Demo currently lives in South Florida, USA and was a millionaire at age 24. He's a thought leader, life strategist and an incredible music maker.

Life-Shaping Events

There are a couple of big events that reshaped my future and changed the trajectory of my life.

The first took place when I was in college. A friend of mine passed away tragically in an accident. He had a small business that he was working on and was doing pretty well. He was so young when he passed, and it triggered me to start really looking at time from a different perspective, where I wanted my place in this world to be and what I wanted success to look like for myself.

I attended his funeral, which was filled with many wonderful people honoring his life. Although he had done so much, there was so much more that he could have done.

It really got me thinking. If I died, what would people say about me? What am I really doing with my life?

I made a firm decision that day that I would play at a bigger level. I didn't know what that looked like and I didn't even know what that really meant at that point, but I knew I had to start doing things differently. I had to go beyond what I was presently doing.

I left college and decided to pursue music, which has always been a passion of mine. I dove in with both feet and the decision I made in that moment really shaped my life moving forward.

The second event that helped shape my future was when I met Timbaland (a record producer, rapper, singer, songwriter and DJ), who ended up becoming one of my main collaborators. I remember the day I met him like it was yesterday.

Years prior to meeting him, I had heard a song on the radio he produced for Missy Elliot called *The Rain*. I remember hearing that song and saying to myself, I want to work with these people.

Fast forward 10 years and here I was in a room with him, working and collaborating together. It blew my mind that I had set the objective to work with them and it actually came to fruition a decade later. It got me thinking, if I could create this opportunity merely by firmly planting the idea in my mind, what else could I create?

Belief

I started realizing, if I really believe that I can have, be or do something, it's not only possible, but likely that I'll achieve it. I took on that understanding from that point forward and ran with it.

When I had this realization, I said, "I'm going to do what I want and I'm just going to go for it like there is no limitation. I'm going to see how far I can go." And I've held the belief ever since that I could do anything I set out to achieve.

I live my life in every moment, as if there's no tomorrow, no next hour, only now.

When I was younger, I swore I was from a different planet because I didn't buy into what I heard most people say to me. Throughout my youth I heard things like, "You can't do that," You shouldn't do that," "That's impossible." I was constantly surrounded by this language and belief and I chose to ignore it.

It seemed like every time I wanted to do something, like join gymnastics, I would make a decision and then I'd say, "I'm going to the state championship." The response I received from those around me would be, "Do you know how difficult that is?"

It was always this constant negative reinforcement and I just never accepted or bought into it. I don't know what exactly possessed me to choose not to think this way, but I'm grateful for it. I chose not to believe there were limitations on things. Admittedly, it got me in a lot of trouble when I was a young man – I just did what I wanted to do in pretty much any situation.

I remember my Mother constantly reminding me that I wasn't being very original when I copied what other people were doing. I really got that in my mind and by the time I was in middle school, I started doing the opposite of what my peers were doing. When the crowd went to the right I'd go left. I went the opposite direction of the masses.

I still do that now. I don't allow anyone else's opinion or belief come close to influencing me. I decide, this is what I'm going to do, and I keep doing it regardless of how my circumstances might appear.

My music career took off fast as I collaborated with powerhouses like Timbaland, Madonna, Jimmy Douglas, and Missy Elliott. Later I made the decision to switch career paths and began surrounding myself with thought leaders like Bob Proctor, Jack Canfield, and Les Brown.

I believe in myself regardless of my circumstances, and I believe that if I really want something I can go out and get it. Every human being has the ability to do that, it's just that they get caught up in what everyone else says and they allow outside opinions and beliefs to influence the decisions they make.

I spend most of my time now teaching people not to care what anyone thinks and act on what it is they really want.

I like to encourage thought-provoking and self-analyzing questions like, if you were going to die in a week, how would you really live your life today?

Most people have this idea that there's an abundance of time and they stroll through life nonchalantly allowing it to just slip by. Many people in my world have passed away over the years and the experience of that has given me a sense of urgency in life. It's too short not to live it with vigor.

Tomorrow is not guaranteed so what can I do today? This seemingly simple question can shift the way you look at life in a big way. Living life as if there's no tomorrow is one of my main beliefs systems and I can tell you from personal experience that it's a great way to live.

Live your life now. Don't take anything for granted. It can all disappear in an instant.

Self-confidence and Failure

Self-confidence is the engine for everything. I believe if you don't have self-confidence, you're never going to reach your potential. As Henry Ford put it, "Whether you think you can or you think you can't, you're right."

There's a scene in Star Wars where Luke attempts to use the force to raise his ship out of the water. He starts to lift it and then fails. Yoda then, frustrated with Luke, uses the force himself to lift the ship out of the water and Luke says, "I don't believe it," and Yoda replies, "That is why you fail." You see, he couldn't do it because he didn't believe it in the first place. Now, I know this is a movie but a good example of what I mean.

For most people, this is the reason they fail. They don't believe they can because they lack confidence in themselves. The funny thing about confidence is that you develop confidence from surviving something. When you take a risk, you get uncomfortable. Every time you put yourself out there and you survive, your confidence builds up stronger and stronger.

The cycle of fear keeps fueling most people. They are scared to fail. Fail is really just an acronym for First Act In Learning. You learn when you fail.

Then, you can make the adjustments and keep building your self-confidence and self-image.

My personal belief is we are spiritual beings. This body is what keeps us here. This body is our vehicle, our home that we're residing in on this journey through life.

Unfortunately, most people don't take care of their body. I like to think of it as a holy temple. You never go into a temple and see trash everywhere. You don't see graffiti on the walls. It's a pristine place and I think that you should care for your body in the same way. You want to be able to look in the mirror and say to yourself, "I look good. I feel good. I can do anything. I'm in great shape and I feel healthy."

When you deliberately think this way about yourself, it fuels confidence. Once you've developed confidence, you really can do anything.

Growing up and money

I didn't grow up in poverty, but we weren't living in abundance either. I grew up in a middle-class household and my parents were well kept with their money. My Father always made sure I had a couple of dollars in my pocket. I developed my beliefs around money merely by watching him put in tons of hours in his work.

When I first began my career in music, I worked like there was no tomorrow and followed that pattern. In one year, I worked 365 days. I spent 345 of them consistently working 14 and 16-hour days. I was really killing myself and I got to the point where I just physically broke down and realised this isn't how it should be.

At that point I started asking the question - How can I earn more money if there's only so much time?

I started meeting people that were earning lots of money and I realised these people weren't working very hard. They weren't doing a lot and yet they were earning a lot.

I learned that if you want to learn how to do something, go find someone who is actually doing it, and doing it well, and ask them to teach you. Until you find they are lying or misleading you in some way, keep doing what they suggest, and you'll win too.

I did that and found out that it wasn't about working harder. It was about providing more service. It was a major breakthrough and discovery for me.

I didn't have to work harder. I just have to figure out how to make the clients feel like "Demo is worth his weight in gold."

When I did that, my approach to serving them changed and the results changed. All of a sudden, I was in the upper echelons.

I was working with big players like Madonna, Beyoncé, Jay Z, Rihanna and more.

At that point I went from making $17K in my first year to almost $40K in my second year. Then in my third year in the music industry, I jumped to almost $350 thousand and way past the million mark soon after.

It happened so fast simply by understanding that one principle. **Money is just a reward for a service rendered so render more service and you're going to get rewarded with more money.**

What a concept. Why had I not learned this up until now? I always thought I had a healthy attitude about money until I started earning more money. I believe you should use money and love people. Most people have that backward – they love money and use people and that comes back to bite them in the end.

You need people to earn money. You can't earn money without some kind of transaction. Get into the idea of providing service, regardless of your field or industry. Really reflect and ask yourself, how can I provide more service? Then take action and make a difference and watch the money come flowing to you.

I do that all the time now. It's one of the primary questions I ask myself throughout the day. How can I provide more service? What can I do to serve the people around me better?

I constantly come from that place and take action on ways to provide more and better service, and the money just shows up.

I achieved my first million at the age of 24 and as I think about it, it truly feels like it was just yesterday. I really thought that there was going to be fireworks and it was going to be this massive thing to celebrate. But it wasn't. It was just another day at the office.

There really is no difference between earning $100K or $1M. I celebrated more the hundred thousand than I did the million. After earning my first hundred thousand, the perspective I ran with was that I just needed to do that 10 more times and I'd hit a million. Once I made it easy in my mind it just happened.

From 2005 to 2007 I worked on countless records and had more number one records than I can tell you. It got to the point where everything Timbaland and I worked together went straight to the top ten, right out of the gate. It was like the Midas touch. Everything we touched turned to gold or platinum in most cases.

It makes me think of what Napoleon Hill said, "When riches begin to come they come so quickly, in such great abundance, that one wonders where they've been hiding during all those lean years."

I remember wondering where was all this abundance of money when I really needed it? It didn't seem that long ago that I was eating rice and living at my Mother's house dreaming of getting out of there.

The millions kept coming and I just thought it could go on forever. But once I had an abundance of money, my perspective changed. I realised I didn't really need a lot of money to be happy. I had a successful career, a big house, a fancy lifestyle, wife, daughter, but I wasn't really happy.

There was something missing from my life and that's when I got into self-development. I've invested almost half a million dollars in my personal development through countless seminars and training. Literally a small fortune over four years of my life committed to attending seminars on a monthly basis – and sometimes even two or three a month.

If I had to choose, **I'd say the best thing about having money is that it gives you the freedom to do whatever you want whenever you want, which is how I've always wanted to live my life.** I now choose to live moderately and for me it's no longer about material things. I've refocused my life to live intentionally into my purpose. And life is so much better when lived that way. I'm driven by something deeper and stronger than ever.

Daily Success Habits

The first thing I do every morning is I take a moment to experience gratitude for simply opening my eyes, because I know one day they won't. Then I jump out of bed and take ten minutes to stretch.

I typically get into the gym right away in the morning and come home and study for about an hour. I also meditate a few times throughout the day for about 10-20 minutes to re-center.

Every night before I go to sleep, I write down my top five goal-achieving activities for the following day so when I wake up I already have an agenda. Sometimes they're not that complicated, they're easy tasks, but they make the list because they move me closer toward my goal.

Mentors

I've had lot of mentors in my life. In my music career, Timbaland helped me to become a producer, Jimmy Douglas helped me develop as an engineer and Madonna as a human being.

In my self-development career, Les Brown has been a speaking mentor. Jack Canfield helped me develop as a trainer and Bob Proctor helped me really figure out what I want to do and be as a teacher. I have been very fortunate to have great mentors.

I would say to anybody who's reading this book, go and find somebody who's doing exactly the same thing that you want to do and ask them to show you how to do it. Unless you find out they're lying or don't know what they're talking about, do as they say.

Recipe for Success

Decide on what you want but, when you decide, take money out of the equation. Pretend you hit the lottery and you came into some money. Now what would you do every day going forward?

What is something you would be really happy about that you would do for free? That's where I would start.

I would design a goal around what you like doing.

I like working with people. I like helping people. I like teaching others about success and how to achieve it. That's what drives me. It's what gets me up every day. It's what gets me to go and put all this time and effort in developing myself, developing presentations and impacting others.

Life is not designed for us to fail it's designed for us to win.

Pick a goal. If you're not really sure, then dabble in something, but start working toward something.

Most people aim at nothing. If you aim at nothing, you're going to hit it right in the middle of the head and you'll get nothing.

You've got to aim at something, so pick something. Then just work every day toward that and be consistent.

Right now, I'm in south Florida and if I wanted to walk to New York City, if I took a few steps a day in that direction, I would at some point get there. Now, if I ran a mile every day I'd get there faster. If I only took one step every day, I'd get there slower. If I ran 50 miles a day I would get there faster.

It doesn't matter how long it takes. **Don't compare yourself to anybody.** Don't worry about what anybody else is doing. Just focus on what you want and then decide this is it. I'm going to commit my life to doing this and work every day toward it. **Do five steps every day toward it and eventually you**'ll get there.

Don't be influenced by what other people say or think. Pick a goal, work toward it and just keep doing it until you get there. It might take me 10 years, it might take you three years it might take the reader 20 years, but who cares as long as you get there.

Just decide what you want and commit to it every day and before you know it, you'll get there!

SUMMARY

- Decide what you want to do. Don't let anyone else's opinion limit you.
- Self-confidence is the engine for everything. Build your confidence and belief.
- Provide more service and the money will flow
- Live life in the present like there's no tomorrow
- Don't compare yourself to anyone else
- Just decide on a goal and start taking action towards it

PART THREE

DAILY RITUALS FOR SUCCESS

"We are what we repeatedly do.
Excellence, then, is not an act, but a habit."
Bob Proctor

Daily Rituals

In this section, I'm going to share a range of success habits that you can introduce and apply to your life straight away.

Daily rituals are an important part of developing your millionaire self-image. Implementing these habits can help you create more of what you love and desire in your life. These rituals continue to enhance your life as they become a part of who you are. They contribute to increasing your confidence, your belief in yourself and who you are.

Make the decision to be highly committed to your success. The more committed you are, the more successful you'll be.

I want to share with you some ideas and strategies that one of my mentors, Peggy McColl, shared with me. I wanted to include them in this book for you, because you'll find them mentioned throughout the previous chapters.

These are some rituals that you can apply to your life, whether you choose to do them every day is up to you.

They don't take a long time, nor are they difficult to do; in fact they're easy to do. You need to make a decision to create these daily habits to rewire your subconscious mind and create new paradigms that serve you.

Get into the habit of growing and stretching yourself. Get into the habit of being committed. That's one of the things that successful people do (remember, I didn't start this way, I had to develop my daily ritual muscle). Successful people develop habits that are consistent, ways of being that set them up for success.

The purpose behind these daily rituals is to achieve something. You want to accomplish something, have something, go somewhere or be something. That's why you do the daily rituals. Make sure you have a clear goal in mind and you're emotionally connected to it. When you start to do these things, they're like the foundations for building your goal from the ground up.

How many people share that they're frustrated because they're not getting results? Quite simply put it's because they don't have these disciplines, they don't have the focus, and they don't enter into the spirit of what they want.

It doesn't matter whether you're doing one or all of these daily rituals for success. What matters most is your feeling. I really want you to get this, what are you focusing on every day? What are you giving your attention to? What you give attention to, will expand and grow.

There's no particular order with the rituals but I am going to start with gratitude.

Gratitude

> "*The whole process of mental adjustment and attunements*
> *can be summed up in one word: Gratitude.*"
> – Wallace Wattles

Being grateful for what you have in your life – the people, and surroundings can change your feelings in an instant. You can also be grateful for things in advance and this helps draw to you more of the things you want.

When creating your millionaire self-image, you can incorporate gratitude into an affirmation like, "I am so happy and grateful now that I have a millionaire self-image." Feel the feeling of gratitude as you're writing, "I am so happy and grateful." This causes you to think of the emotion and anchor it into your system. What does it feel like for you to have that abundance and prosperity? You may have something that is the same every day.

You can write a gratitude statement relevant to your business or financial relationship, your health or any area of your life. You can give gratitude for anything and everything. Thinking about and giving genuine thanks creates a shift in your feeling.

You can write a gratitude list of 10 things every day that you're grateful for and make this a daily practice. You can do this first thing in the morning or before your head hits the pillow in the evening. Remember the purpose of being grateful is to create the feeling.

From my experience, when I write my gratitude it keeps me in my head, but when I think it, I really feel it. I weave gratitude throughout my day. Work out what's most effective for you and create the habit of daily gratitude.

You could also write out a statement multiple times a day that really giving focus to a particular statement (i.e. 100 x day). Here are some examples:

I am so happy and grateful now that I own my ideal home.

I am so happy and grateful now that my annual income is my monthly or weekly income.

I am so happy and grateful ...

When you write it out multiple times every single day, it causes you to think and feel the emotion as you impress it over and over on your conscious and subconscious mind. The key is to feel good. If you are feeling frustrated about what you're doing, rushing it or find it a tedious process, that's the opposite of its purpose. Stop and get yourself into the right mindset and feeling. You want to really connect with it and feel good. It's not a matter of writing the gratitude, it's how are you feeling and connect with it when writing the gratitude.

As a daily ritual it must be felt genuinely in your heart.

Affirmations

Your subconscious mind can only accept information. It can't reject it. Positive or negative thoughts will both be accepted. For many of you, your inner thoughts are negative and the purpose of using affirmations is to change them to the thoughts you want to be having. I wasn't even aware of some of the thoughts that I was having, they were deeply embedded in my subconscious mind and controlling my results on the outside. Writing, reading and saying affirmations is the process of reprogramming your mind. It's as if you already have it through repetition. It doesn't matter what you're saying it's simply to invoke positive thoughts and to feel certain emotions.

You can write the same statement over and over in a journal. Record affirmations on a voice loop (an app) or ThinkUp (an app for positive affirmations) on your phone and listen to them over and over. You can put them on cards and sticky notes around the house or in the car where you'll see them. You can even laminate them and put them in the shower.

They'll make no difference though, unless you read them, say them out loud, listen to them or write them and really feel them. You have to action the process of using the affirmation.

Affirm and genuinely feel it. – There's a difference.

My experience with affirmations in the beginning was that I would write them out and go through the motions, not allowing myself to really connect with the words and what they meant to me. I recognised this and had to really pay attention to my affirmations and the feeling I wanted to connect with. It can help when you use emotionally charged words in your affirmations. For example, "I am a powerhouse," "I am strongly confident," "I am awesome at…" "I am incredibly successful."

Really pay attention to what you're saying or writing. A word that doesn't make you feel good can cancel out anything you're saying. You could have one word in an affirmation that's counter-productive. For example, I am debt free. You want to remove the word debt, otherwise that's what your subconscious mind will focus on and you'll get more of it. You want the train of thought to be, "I am financially free."

Affirmation examples

- Money is forever flowing freely in my life and there's always a divine surplus (how does that feel for you, that there's always a divine surplus?). Don't just read it for the sake of it. You're reading it to cause something, to feel something. The feeling is key.

- I am moving forward financially

- I have all the time I need and it feels great!

- I always have plenty of money to do whatever I want to do

- I am happy, healthy and wealthy. Thank you! It is so.

- I attract success and abundance into my life because that's who I am. I am success. I am abundance.

Tips

1) Find affirmations that are positive only and have emotionally charged words.

2) When you say your affirmations, say them with emotion and conviction so you attach yourself to the feeling state.

3) Look yourself in the eye with lots of energy and repeat your affirmations with lots of emotion in front of the mirror.

4) I've recently added listening to Epic music (do a YouTube search) when saying my affirmations, and this has been a great way of connecting with my feelings.

Goal Card

Set yourself a big goal and then write it on a card and take it with you everywhere. A goal that you have absolutely no idea how you're going to achieve, but it's something that you really, really want. It excites you and scares you at the same time. The reason for writing it on the card, carrying it everywhere and looking at it, is to continually remind you to focus on it.

When setting this goal ask yourself a few questions.

Do your goals belong to you or do they belong to someone else?

If you have goals set already, are your current goals making you excited or energized?

This is very important. Take the time to connect yourself with the feeling and the goal that you want. This is critical.

Have your goal card with you every single day and look at it, read and say it regularly – fall in love with your goal. Feel the gratitude of the goal already being materialized into physical reality. The purpose of the goal card is to connect you with the feeling of already having that goal – seeing and feeling that goal now.

Goal & Date completed _____

I'm so happy and grateful now that…

_____

_____

_____

Here's an example of a statement for your goal card:

I am so happy and grateful now that I am earning a minimum of $200,000 every single month. I love it. I am happy, healthy and wealthy. Thank you. It is so.

You want to make sure that you follow a few rules:

- Keep it in the present
- Set a date (you don't know how long it will take, sometimes more, sometimes less). There's a law of gestation – say 14-21 days for a carrot seed to germinate, 280 days for a baby, for your goal you really don't know.

The goal card becomes the boss of how you want your life to actually be. When you achieve that goal, set another one about how you want to be living that life of yours and what you want to be achieving.

Visualisation

This is a daily exercise. This was something I wasn't really good at. I had to develop my will and focus muscle to choose the picture in my mind that was associated with my goal. You have to focus your conscious attention to keep the picture on the screen of your mind, on the good that you desire.

A great time to do this is when you're relaxed, as in first thing when you wake up and when you go to sleep. You can set an alarm and remind yourself to get quiet and visualise for 2, 5 or 10 minutes. It doesn't matter how long you do it. What's most important is how you are feeling.

Get into the habit of visualizing everyday (you're doing it anyway whether you realise it or not). The purpose of actively visualising is to focus on how you want your life to be. To create that movie in your mind.

Visualisation can take many forms. It could be done in a spontaneous way like active visualization. This is walking around in your home, but using your imagination to see what you want to see. i.e. your new kitchen, the new house you want, the renovations you want, your new car in the driveway or the money in your bank account. You can also see yourself driving down the road in a particular car, putting your key in the door and opening your dream home. You're actively involved in visualizing a particular outcome with physical movement. Or you can be sitting in your chair or lying in your bed visualizing yourself in your future home, seeing your bank account as you'd like it, being on holiday with your loved ones etc.

Neville Goddard, the author of "The Power of Awareness," shares a story that when he was in Barbados, he really wanted to leave to go to New York City, but was told there was no room on the ship. Further , he was told there was a waiting list and it was going to take six months to be New York bound. He ignored this and practiced active visualization, seeing his name on the list for a ship departing leaving Barbados and heading to New York. There was a ship leaving in a couple of days.

Regardless of the fact, that the ship was completely booked there was a waiting list, his name was at the bottom of that waiting list, and he'd been told it would take six months to get aboard, he actively visualised that he had his stuffed pack walking up the gangplank. He saw himself on the ship. He could feel the sea air on his face, he could smell the salt in the sea, he could feel the mist of the ocean on deck.

Goddard felt it, lived it and visualised it over and over. Within a few days, he got a phone call saying he and his family, were on the ship. None of the physical evidence pointed that way, but he practiced the visualisation technique and believed he'd be on that ship.

You can use this technique for parking spots, money in your bank account, a new house, relationships or your health. You can use it for anything you want. If you can see it in your mind, you can hold it in your hand. The key for this to work is you have to feel it with your senses and you have to believe it.

I followed the recording of Sandy Gallagher's (see reference section for this) on visualisation and studied the book "The Invisible Power" by Genevieve Behrand. I had a lot of resistance from my paradigms telling me that I couldn't visualise. The stories are priceless when you become aware of them. I created a mind movie (mindmovie.com) on my computer using pictures from my vision board which helped me to see the visual on the outside in picture form and listen to music with it. Then I was able to internalize it and play the same pictures in my mind. Be persistent because it really works.

In a nutshell, the science behind visualisation tells us the reason it works so well is that your mental rehearsal of a task has the same effect as physically performing the task (i.e. the same neural connections and pathways fire up whether you're actually doing the task or just visualizing yourself doing the task). Don't take my word for it, do your own research.

Your mind starts creating a pattern or mental script for the task with regular visualization, and this script kicks into play when you next go out to actually do the task. Creating this clear mental picture is a critical step to fulfilling your goals.

When you imagine yourself being successful and engage your emotions, you create a neural network (a network of brain cells) of that image in your mind. The energy of the images you create causes your body to vibrate at a cellular level.

Frequently visualising this scene impresses the image onto your sub-conscious. Your brain starts looking for things in the physical world that match these images… so they become automatically attracted to the right opportunities when they come your way. Dr Joe Dispenza goes into great depth explaining the science behind changing your mind.

Questions

Asking yourself questions causes you to think and feel emotion and causes your brain to search for the answers. This is a great tool to use. You want powerful, positive questions. Even if you don't get an answer right away, when you ask the question, your brain goes work figuring it out. Ask questions that cause you to experience the emotion of already having achieved your goal. When you're thinking about what you want, you really want to be feeling the emotions of already having it. This definitely speeds its delivery.

Here are some questions to ask yourself:

- What is it that you'd love to have be or do? What does that feel like?
- Now that you've succeeded how does it feel?
- Now that you have that, how does it feel?
- Now that you're doing that, how does it feel?
- Now that you've accomplished that, how does it feel?

Be really aware and notice anytime you're in destructive mode. Be hyper-aware. Quite often we ask ourselves disempowering questions rather than empowering questions. (i.e. Why can't I do this? versus What can I do next?) Develop a heightened awareness when you're feeling those destructive emotions of fear lack of faith, frustration. They'll stop you from achieving any goal. They do this by minimizing your confidence and belief – two critical components of the success of achieving any goal.

Here are more open-ended questions to ask yourself:

• Why am I so successful?

• Why have I attracted the love of my life?

• Why do I look so good?

• Why do I attract the most amazing clients?

• Why is my business generating so much money?

• Why do I have such an amazing partner?

• Why do I have such great health?

• Why do I feel so good?

• Why have I got such a great relationship with money?

• Why is it so easy for me to attract money?

• Why do I have all the money I want and more?

• Why do I earn millions of dollars in revenue doing work that I love?

• What can I do next to improve my income?

I've recorded my questions and listen to them every day.

Why is it that my monthly income increases every month and exceeds my annual income from last year?

You can record your questions and listen to them. Hearing your own voice this way is another powerful tool to access your subconscious mind to give you the answers you're seeking.

Power Life Script

This is where you write a description of you living your ideal life in the present tense. You record it, then listen to it at least once every day – It can be 15 - 20 minutes long. You can use something like voice loop and play it over and over. Peggy McColl is the queen of this and shares this is the one technique that made the biggest difference in her life.

Call it something like "My wonderful life," put it on voice loop and keep it on your phone. It can be playing all the time when you're getting ready in the morning, making dinner, doing the dishes, have air pods in your ears, while walking dogs and before going to bed. It's a similar technique to visualisation as it is impressing images and words over and over in your subconscious mind through autosuggestion. It works so well and it's so easy to do.

Accomplishment/Win List

This is a list of things you've accomplished. You create this for the week, the day, the month. I have a journal that I keep and write my wins in each week and share them with my mastermind group. You can write down things that you're grateful for that you've accomplished. Focus on doing things that are taking you closer to your goals. It really gets you to pay attention to what you're doing rather than what you aren't doing. It's a great way to get you to focus on your wins.

Accountability Partner

Having an accountability partner is a great way to increase your accountability. You can do this one-on-one or as part of a mastermind group.

In a study conducted by Brigham Young University in 1993, it was found that those who set a specific time to share their progress with someone else, had a 95% chance of change. (Source: "It's not about the money," Bob Proctor).

"Every week send each other a list of your tasks that you want to achieve for the week. Every day have this list in front of you. Focus on accomplishing these things. You become consciously aware of them when you're seeing them daily and when you have shared them with an accountability partner. When I'm thinking of my accomplishments, I have them as action items in my agenda or as six daily actions.

I'm great at keeping others accountable, but I've only just found someone that has stepped that up for me to a whole new level. I had to watch some webinars that I'd been resisting watching for months. My accountability partner wouldn't help me any further until I had watched these two webinars within a week. This made me watch them.

Mastermind Group

Form a mastermind group. This is a group of 5-8 people who meet on a weekly basis. You follow a strict meeting agenda and come with wins and a list of wants. You are there to help one another in the group and to hold each other accountable to the tasks that you set yourselves. I had also sought help from my mastermind group that encouraged me to raise my prices. I never would've done this without the support and accountability of my Mastermind group.

Daily Action List

There's a story in "Think and Grow Rich" where a business was being run by a productivity expert. He used a technique that's really going to improve your productivity.

Each day the employees had to write down six things they were going to do the following day. Don't move to the next item until you've finished the one before it. This impacted the business's profits in a big way. I've implemented this in my business and I know that Demo and Jackie referenced this in their stories. Bob Proctor writes his list of six things on a card which also has James Allen's Serenity prayer.

Pre-Sleep

There were studies done that found what you think about before you go to bed creates a better retention rate. Whatever you're thinking about just before you drift off to sleep determines what's showing up most in your life. Neville Goddard talked about it as did Wayne Dyer. It's called Pre-sleep moments. You can create them as focused moments with an index card so you remember. You can ask yourself key questions. You can make up a sign and put it beside your bed "Your Dream is Fulfilled."

Reminders

You can write your affirmations, goals or key phrases on sticky notes or little cards and put them all over your house. They can go in the bathroom, your bedroom, dashboard of your car, on your computer, in your purse/ wallet. The purpose is to have them in front of you as constant reminders.

Alarms on phone/ Reminders

This is a great tool to use instead of just getting you out of bed in the morning. You can set reminders/alarms on your phone for a variety of things. Set your alarm five times throughout the day and check in with how you're feeling. You can do the same process to check in with what thoughts you're having. You can use reminders that you set yourself throughout the day for goal statements or affirmations that prompt you to think of them or say them. For example, "I am so happy and grateful now that …"

You can schedule these into your phone for a particular time every day. This is a great way to keep yourself on track and check in with yourself. I recommend this regularly to the people I work with.

Learn to Laugh

Laughter really is the best medicine. It's so good for your mindset and great for your health. It releases **endorphins** into the body. Endorphins are brain chemicals known as neurotransmitters. These "feel good" chemicals transmit electrical signals within the nervous system. … **They** interact with the opiate receptors in the brain to reduce our perception of pain and act as a natural form of morphine in the body.

Do things every day that cause you to feel good – read jokes, tell jokes, watch funny stuff, catch up with friends who you know you'll have a good laughing session with.

Norman Cousins, the author of "Anatomy of an Illness," had a prognosis that he was going to die and he decided that wasn't going to happen. He was going to find a way to live. He decided to watch all these episodes of "Candid Camera," over and over and watch things that caused him to laugh. He laughed every single day. He laughed his way back to health. There are numerous examples of this where laughter has been the "best medicine." It really allows you to feel good. This one is easy to create as a daily ritual.

Exercise

People who take care of their physical bodies generally do better because they feel better.

There's no denying the importance of exercise. Scheduling this into your daily/weekly routine is a must. Healthy body, healthy mind. Be disciplined in this area. Find something that you enjoy doing, whether it's on your own or with a fitness group. Have a goal in mind for yourself as well. When you exercise your body, it releases feel good hormones called endorphins. If this is something you resist, make an investment in a personal trainer or get an accountability person to exercise with you. You're more likely to work out with a partner.

Self-confidence Formula

As we discussed earlier, you can't outperform your self-image and your confidence is another key to success. When you're repeating this formula daily, you're using the process of autosuggestion: telling your mind over and over what you want it to do.

- Know what you want more than anything else
- Set a date by which you intend to have it
- Sign your name to the formula
- Commit it to memory
- Repeat it aloud once a day
- Have full faith that it will gradually influence your thoughts and actions

Now my own personal experience with this was I had this all outlined and ready to go and I would manage to stick with it for one or two days at a time and then quit.

I did this for years until I learned about paradigms. When I made the decision to do this daily, I made a committed decision realizing that I had to be self-disciplined, give myself the command and follow it. At the time of writing this book, I've managed 11 months straight without missing a day and the self-confidence formula has become an integral part of my day. When you realise it only takes 1min and 50 sec to say it aloud, you realise it's not a difficult thing to do.

This is taken from the book "Think Rich Grow Rich" by Napoleon Hill (a must read). Repeat this daily out loud.

1. I know that I have the ability to achieve my definite purpose in life. Therefore, I demand of myself persistent, continuous action toward its attainment and I here and now promise to render such action.

2. The dominating thoughts of my mind will eventually reproduce themselves in outward physical action and gradually transform themselves into physical reality. Therefore, I will concentrate my thoughts for 30 minutes daily upon the task of thinking of the person that I intend to become. Thereby creating in my mind a clear mental picture.

3. I know through the principle of autosuggestion, any desire that I persistently hold in my mind will eventually seek some expression through some practical means of obtaining the object or position I desire.

4. I have clearly written down a description of my definite chief aim and I will never stop trying until I develop sufficient self-confidence for its attainment.

5. I fully realise that no wealth or position can long endure unless built upon truth and justice. Therefore, I will engage in no transaction that will not benefit all whom it effects. I will succeed by attracting to myself the forces that I wish to use and the cooperation of other people. I will induce others to serve me because of my willingness to serve them. I will eliminate hatred, envy, jealousy, selfishness and cynicism by developing love for all humanity for I know that a negative attitude toward others will never bring me success. I will cause others to believe in me because I will believe in them and in myself.

I will sign my name to this formula, commit it to memory and repeat it aloud once a day in full faith that it will gradually influence my thoughts and actions, so I will become a self-reliant and successful person.

Name _____ Date _____

Study

Bob Proctor shares that there are only two ways to change a paradigm; one is through an emotional impact, which is usually negative, the other is through constant, spaced repetition. The constant, spaced repetition of study, autosuggestion and application of the study (taking action) will expand your awareness. He encourages study every single day. Study from the great books, find a mentor and listen to recordings over and over.

I've studied something every day consistently for the past three years, and made the choice to get up earlier than the rest of the house so I have peace and quiet. Let me help you so you don't make the mistakes I did.

Although I was dedicated, focused and absorbed in this personal study, I was very much in my intellectual mind. I was doing the study for the sake of the study and therefore my results really didn't change that much in the beginning. I was also doing a lot of study which kind of overwhelmed me and didn't allow me to focus on changing one paradigm at a time. I needed to internalize the material. When I made the switch to thinking about my goal and how to apply what I was studying to everything that I was doing and wanting in my life, and taking action - everything changed. I started with my self-image paradigm, then began on my money paradigm and my relationships paradigm as I was building my business.

I have added some recommended study material at the end of the book.

Read with others

Read every day with another person – this causes you to really concentrate on what you're reading and dig deeper into the material. Choose a specific time every day and read with a purpose in mind so that you're focusing on your goal. This is something that definitely sounds illogical. When you're reading, continually have your specific goal in mind. Reading the same material every day is profound. It's the process of repetition of the material and increasing your awareness that will make a difference with this ritual. I get on a call every day and read a chapter of a book. You can do 30 or 90 day challenges, or just choose a chapter from a book. The important thing is not to go through the motions everyday, but to immerse yourself in what you're reading and apply it to your goal. When you're reading ask yourself, Am I applying this? How would this get me closer to my goal? How could I apply this to my goal?

Meditation

Sitting quietly for 20 minutes – that's your goal. You can begin by sitting quietly for five minutes. The process of stillness, of getting calm and relaxed is giving yourself the opportunity to really connect with yourself; the spirit side. We focus so much on the physical and our intellect and five senses. This quieting of the mind allows us to use our intellectual faculties of intuition and be guided by within. There's so much material on this. I use a daily practice each morning where I spend five mins before the start of the day sitting still and asking for guidance for the day in a calm and relaxed state. It's not a matter of how long or how often you do it in a day, more that you make it a regular practice.

This has been proven to be so healthy by Dr. Joseph Murphy – it's the quiet mind that gets things done.

Vision Board

A vision board is a series of images or pictures of things that you want in your life. It could be a vacation, a boat, flying business class, a new car, a new relationship or a certain amount of money.

The idea is that the pictures trigger a feeling within you about what it will feel like when you achieve your goals. Put a photo of yourself in as many of the pictures as you can. I cut out a picture of myself and put myself in first class for my next trip to Canada. I wanted to be in Bob Proctor's Inner Circle, so I had a badge made up and used my picture with Bob to create this. I created a book cover with best-selling international author on it. I have a picture of the house I want to buy. What are some pictures that you could put on a board right away? The bigger the better. Take the time to enjoy this process of setting it up and have fun with it. Then take time each day to look at it and imagine your life experiencing and having those things.

As the mind sees in pictures, it's a great way to impress these images over and over into the subconscious mind and connect with the feeling that you already have them. I have my vision board set up just behind my computer so that I'm focusing on it every day. I've had to upgrade my photos as I've achieved so many of them in the last six months.

SUMMARY

"Discipline is the ability to give yourself a command and follow it."
Bob Proctor

What you're doing is not the important part – it's how you are feeling that's the key. Doing things in a certain way. The idea behind all these principles is to put yourself into the emotional state so that you are feeling as if, acting as if, so that you are living as if you already have everything you desire.

That's the idea behind all the daily rituals for success.

When you're focusing on your goal each day, you're working with the natural laws of the Universe – they're there to support you. You are invoking the laws, connecting to the laws and working with the laws, rather than against them. You're attracting to you everything that's requisite for the fulfillment of your desire.

Now if this all sounds a bit out there– that's okay – it did to me too when I first started. BUT- it's like electricity – we use it, we don't know how it works, we just flick a light switch on and there's light. It's like our five senses, we use them but do we really know how they work? There are laws of nature – i.e. we know about gravity. I want you to be as successful in the least amount of time possible. I want you to start working with the laws rather than against them. Choose the habits that resonate with you.

With each of these daily rituals it's a choice of what resonates with you and then whether or not you consistently do them. All the results present in your life right now are a result of your previous thinking. These success rituals will help you to get your thoughts, feelings and actions into alignment and focus on the good that you desire – but it doesn't happen overnight. Remember the law of germination. Evidence of them working may not appear right away. If you can imagine, it's a bit like going to the gym, your abdominal muscles don't just appear overnight. You've got to do the work.

"Absence of evidence is not evidence of absence."

Bob Proctor

You may have thoughts that these exercises are silly or illogical and that's okay. Remember, you're upgrading your subconscious mind with a lot of these tools and dealing with your paradigm.

Repetition of these daily rituals is causing the reprogramming of your subconscious mind through autosuggestion. That's where our beliefs are held, our paradigms. The feeling/emotional part of our mind. Once you take inspired action, your habits and behaviours will change. This, in turn, will cause you to take different actions, thereby creating the results you want. Simple. But only 1 % of the population will choose to make these changes – will it be you?

AFTERWORD

You are destined for success. You have a choice.

Break free of your paradigms, your limitations.

You have infinite potential.

Use the stories and the tools in this book to inspire and guide you.

Everything you believe is true.

Choose to believe anything is possible.

ABOUT THE AUTHOR

Rachael began her career in hospitality, agriculture and as a teacher. For 15 years she had the privilege to teach and inspire students from K-12 and helped her husband run his agricultural operation. She branched out into educational consultancy and leadership before beginning her mentoring and coaching business.

Alongside raising her four children, Rachael joined the Proctor Gallagher Institute in 2016 to work alongside Bob Proctor and help to "wake up the world" to what is really possible.

She's passionate about helping others achieve success and transforming the paradigms and self-image of adults and children to allow them to become the best version of themselves.

Be mentored by Rachael

Contact Details

rachael@rachaeldownie.com.au

+61427 861 202 to arrange a time

www.rachaeldownie.com.au

REFERENCES

Links

University of Texas at Austin 2014 Commencement Address – Admiral William H. McRaven Texas , https://youtu.be/KgzLzbd-zT4

Medical Author: Melissa Conrad Stoppler MD https://www.medicinenet.com/script/main/art.asp?articlekey=55001

How Your Self-Image Determines Your Success | T. Harv Eker http://blog.harveker.com/self-image/ accessed 26th Nov 2017

http://blog.harveker.com/get-rich/ (2)
Barbara Bush, Address to Kennebunk (Maine) High School, source unknown

Peggy McColl Transcribed Streaming Review January 2018

Books

Allen, James., *As a Man Thinketh*, Originally published 1902 Chapter Serenity, 2019.

Behrend, Genevieve., *The Invisible Power* (2013), Rough Draft Publishing.

Cousins, Norman., *Anatomy of an Illness as Perceived by the Patient : Reflections on Healing and Regeneration.* (New York Norton, 1979).

Dispenza, Dr Joe., *Breaking the Habit of Being Yourself*, (Hay House, 2012).

Hill, Napolean.,*Think and Grow Rich* (71st Anniversary Addition, The Ralston Society , 1938).

Proctor, Bob., *You were Born Rich* (McCrary Publishing, 1984).

Wattles, D. Wallace.,*The Science of Getting Rich. Your Master Key to Success*, (2009).

Extra Resources/ What's Next?

- ThinkUp app – abundance affirmations
- Voice Loop - Record your written millionaire self-image and play it daily on repeat.
- Secret Money App Listen to Bob Proctor's money affirmation https://www.youtube.com/watch?v=KkFtcQUHO9w
- Sandy Gallagher Visualisation Audio https://www.youtube.com/watch?v=E50dYv3bnFk

PROGRAMS

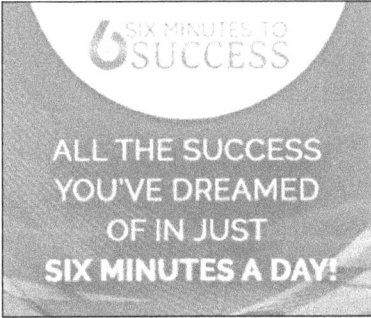

Six Minutes to Success Overview

Dramatically increase your results – In ALL areas of your life with the ease, convenience and motivation of Six Minutes to Success. Get practical steps combined with the real inspiration you need to earn more money, create thriving relationships, start a wildly successful business, lose any amount of weight and live a more productive, fulfilling life.

Excellent For …
…anyone and everyone looking to improve their life.
http://bit.ly/6msuccessr

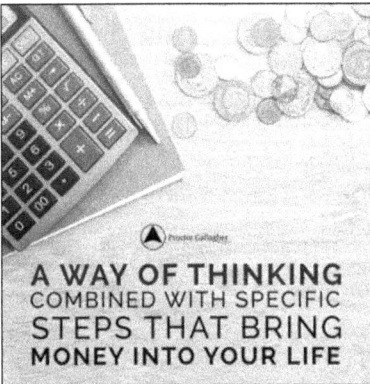

Science of Getting Rich Program Overview

Get rich in a predictable and reliable way with The Science of Getting Rich. Enjoy more abundance, joy and wealth without working harder or giving up all your time.

The Science of Getting Rich is quite possibly the most impactful personal development program. It teaches the foundations of personal development, the law of attraction and achieving the life you really want. As such, it can teach you how to execute and achieve any goal with precision and accuracy.

Excellent For ...
People who have a pressing need or strong desire for money... anyone who hasn't found the time or opportunity to go deeply into the study of metaphysics... and those who are willing to take the conclusions of science as a basis for action.
http://bit.ly/sciencegetrichr

UNDERSTAND ALL OF THE LAWS THAT GOVERN YOUR RESULTS EACH DAY

Working With the Law Program Overview

Create the life you really want by understanding and applying the laws of the universe. Like gravity, these laws are always at work in your life, dictating the results you get each day.

Working With the Law was developed by Bob Proctor and Mary Morrissey, two leaders in the personal development field. This in-depth program examines the Universal Laws that govern the results we get in life.

In addition to explaining the Law of Attraction, this program examines each of the other equally important laws that govern our daily lives (11 total). Bob often refers to these laws as forgotten, because they are not very well known to the modern world, even though they've been around since the beginning of time.

Excellent For ...
People who are interested in the Law of Attraction... anyone who wants to know more about Universal Laws... and everyone looking to improve their life.
http://bit.ly/withthelawr

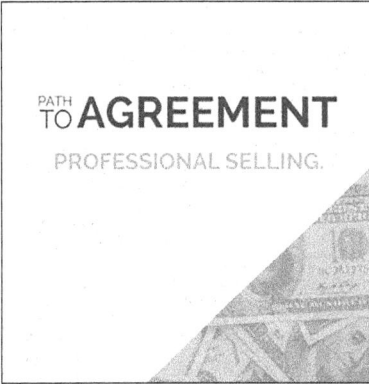

Path to Agreement Professional Selling Overview

Sales is the highest paid profession in the world. However, most salespeople don't understand that selling is all in the mind.

In *Path to Agreement*, you'll discover a proven six-step mental process anyone can use to earn any amount they want. It shows you that selling is not talking to people about a product or service. It's not being pushy, aggressive, or competitive. It's not one person winning and the other losing.

Professional selling is a win-win proposition. It's leading a prospect down a path of agreement. It's finding out something they want, mixing it with something you have and then giving it back to them.

Excellent For …
People who work on commission… anyone who would like to become a highly paid salesperson… and business owners and aspiring business owners who want to create a thriving enterprise.

http://bit.ly/pathwayagreer

ALL THE SUCCESS
YOU'VE EVER
DREAMED OF ...
MAGICALLY YOURS!

Magic in your Mind Overview

In just six weeks, you'll discover how to…

- Move beyond mere mental activity to real thinking.
- Originate thoughts that vibrate in harmony with who you want to be, do and have.
- Consciously use your imagination to purposely bring your goals to life and create a life that looks exactly the way you want it to look.
- Project forward and create memories of a future event that is beyond the point where your wish has come true.
- Transform any challenge by changing your perception of the situation.
- Transform your hopes and wishes for what you MIGHT into expectations of what you WILL have.
- And much more!

Excellent For …

… anyone and everyone looking to improve their life.

http://bit.ly/magicmindr

The New Lead the Field Coaching Program Overview

Make your income match your dreams and break away from your habitual way of living with The New Lead the Field Coaching program! Over the course of just 4 months (120 days) you will begin to earn more money, enjoy more freedom and experience deeper more meaningful relationships.

In this New Lead the Field Coaching Program, Bob Proctor and Sandy Gallagher will assist you in expanding your level of awareness by sharing the ancient truths and laws that Earl Nightingale so brilliantly buried in this award-winning personal development series of recordings.

They explain how and why universal laws govern your life. Your success is going to accelerate as you expose yourself to these 12 mind-expanding, life-enhancing, explosive and relevant segments.

Excellent For ...
... anyone and everyone looking to improve their life.
http://bit.ly/leadthefieldr

Living the Legacy Overview

Living the Legacy fills a unique and enormous need in the personal development industry. It reveals the secret golden thread to success that Napoleon Hill wove throughout *Think and Grow Rich*—the book that is responsible for creating countless millionaires. Living the Legacy is a high-quality, movie-style production that takes you on a journey through Think and Grow Rich like never before.

Excellent For ...

Anyone who loves *Think and Grow Rich* but hasn't quite cracked the code to success... people who have a strong desire for money... anyone who wants to improve the quality of their life.

http://bit.ly/livinglegacyr

Paradigm Shift Event Overview

Paradigms are mental programs that have almost exclusive control over our habitual behaviour … and almost all of our behaviour is habitual.

They control the way you view yourself, the world and opportunity. They control how you approach change and challenges. They control your success and happiness in life. Paradigms are who you are.

A Paradigm Shift is the only way to bridge the gap between how you're currently living and how you want to live.

Bob Proctor has been teaching people the various aspects of changing their paradigm for more than 40 years.

And now he is teaching the entire process at a seminar called *Paradigm Shift* on

You'll discover how to:

- Identify your paradigms
- Replace a paradigm that doesn't serve you well with a new one that frees you to create the life you really want
- Transform your finances, health, and lifestyle

Excellent For …
… anyone and everyone looking to improve their life.
http://bit.ly/paradigmshiftr

UNSTOPPABLE FOUNDATION

Empowering Lives Through Education

The Unstoppable Foundation is a non-profit humanitarian organization bringing sustainable education to children and communities in developing countries, thereby creating a safer and more just world for everyone.

The Sponsor a Village Program is at the core of our 5-Pillar development model, in which we not only build schools, but also provide the entire community with access to clean water & sanitation, food & nutrition, healthcare and training for the parents to develop an income. The goal is that each community is self-sustaining within 5 years of implementation.

Private Donors and Sponsors fund the operating costs so that 100% of your donation will go directly to support the international programs.

Please donate here https://unstoppablefoundation.org